Social Change and Violence

The Indian Experience

Social Change and Violence

The Indian Experience

P. R. Rajgopal

Under the Auspices of
Centre for Policy Research

UPPAL PUBLISHING HOUSE
NEW DELHI-110002

UPPAL PUBLISHING HOUSE
3, Ansari Road, Daryaganj, New Delhi-110002

First Published, 1987

ISBN 81-85024-27-8

PRINTED IN INDIA
Published by B.S. Uppal for Uppal Publishing House, New Delhi and Phototypeset by Ess Bee Printers, B-17, Sector-8, NOIDA and Printed at Efficient Offset Printers, New Delhi-28.

Foreword

The Centre for Policy Research has been engaged in the study of violence and its roots over the last two years or so. As the societal transformation moves on in India, the level of violence seems to escalate. Even so the problem is obviously not new either to the world or to India itself. Violence has been endemic in many countries and in many civilizations.

In India itself, Gautam the Budhdha and Mahavir Jain devoted and built most of their religious and spiritual thought around non-violence. Both had profound influence on Mahatma Gandhi and the Indian freedom movement.

Yet, as the wheels of economic, social and political developments have moved on, especially since independence, so has the level of violence. Is it a cancer of the Indian society or is merely a symbol of the process of societal readjustments? Is violence going to eat up the vitals of the Indian society or will it merely act as a catalyst or an inevitable part of the change process?

This study is the second in the series on violence by Shri P R Rajgopal. As a distinguished police official, Shri Rajgopal has seen the various faces of violence at first hand. In the present study, he has examined the variety of socio-economic factors which lead to violence. Policy makers as well as lay citizens will find his practical insights useful in understanding the phenomenon.

Centre for policy Research
New Delhi

V A Pai Panandiker
Director.

PREFACE

It is difficult to compartmentalise neatly a subject such as social change and violence in India without an overlap of the different elements that constitute this complex subject. Even so, an attempt has been made to present this study in five separate parts. In the first part, an attempt has been made to conceptualise violence that this study seeks to project. This study has tried to go beyond mere manifest violence into areas of economic exploitation, violation of human rights and affront to human dignity. In the process it has touched on subjects which may be seen to be outside the scope of a study on violence. But as I view it, violence latent in these areas of human behaviour is far more malignant and sustained than manifest violence which is, in the very nature of it, self limiting. The second part deals with the socio-economic disabilities suffered by very large sections of our population who have been at the receiving end of a type of latent violence that is referred to both in the first and in the second parts. A brief educational and employment profile of the Scheduled Castes and Scheduled Tribes has also been attempted in statistical terms which should give an idea of the efforts that the state governments have made and the measure of success that they have been able to achieve in this field. An effort has also been made to discuss briefly the inadequacy of the institutional infrastructure for resolving the conflicts that have been the inevitable concomitants of social change. The third part deals with the gap between the promises made by the Government and their implementation in respect of the several aspects of agrarian reforms. This has relevance to land reforms, tenurial rights and minimum wages. Arousing hopes without fulfilling them creates a crisis of expectation and an atmosphere in which violence breeds easily. The agrarian reforms have been dealt with in the context of the States of Bihar, Uttar Pradesh, Gujarat and West Bengal. The fourth part illustrates with specific instances, the nature and variety of violence that have characterised the States of

Bihar, Uttar Pradesh, Maharashtra, Karnataka and Gujarat. The fifth and the last part delineates the broad conclusions that flow from the study of violence in the various states in different contexts. Admittedly, these conclusions are of a general nature based on case studies drawn from only a few of the states in the country, and not from all the states. Even this limited study took over fifteen months.

The nature of the study demanded that I identify and focus on the dark areas of administrative failures that resulted in violence in some of the states. Nevertheless this does not in any way detract from several achievements which the country can legitimately be proud of and which have been achieved not through force or coercion by the State but through some of the most desirable democratic processes attempted anywhere in the world.

Certain parts of this study may make distressing reading. These have been deliberately highlighted in the belief that we can do better in these areas, given the necessary political and administrative will, which may have been temporarily weakened by the influence of vested interests. My simple thesis is that geographically a vast country like India with its exploding population, having wrought the social change that it has, through democratic planning process should be an example to many countries where undiluted state dictatorship have failed to pro duce comparable developmental results. Even in those parts of our country which have been disfigured by violence, it should have been possible to redeem the situation if only we had made the necessary administrative and institutional innovations to cope with the demands arising out of social change. It is still not too late to make such an attempt.

The most important and urgently needed institutional reform that the study unfailingly points to concerns the Criminal Justice System. The inherent infirmities and inadequacies of this system are the subject matter of a separate study which I have undertaken as the third part of the overall

Research Study on Violence sponsored by the Centre for Policy Research, New Delhi. The first part was published under the title 'Communal Violence in India'; this is the second part; and the third part will be published under the title. 'Violence and Response', A critique of the Indian Criminal Justice System.

I am deeply grateful to Dr. V.A. Pai Panandiker, the Director of the Centre for Policy Research for his ever willing and generous help in all matters connected with this study. Several friends have contributed their time and labour to make this study what it has come to be in the present form. I thank them all. A special word of thanks to Mr. L.P. Singh, who helped me with some very valuable suggestions and ideas which figure in this study, and also for painstakingly reading through the draft of this text.

I am extremely grateful to S.P. Mathur for helping me in several ways in compiling and processing the material contained in this study. I alone am responsible for the views expressed in the study.

P.R. RAJGOPAL

Contents

PART-V

PART I

CHAPTER 1

CONCEPT OF VIOLENCE IN THE INDIAN CONTEXT

Indian history abounds in illustrious men who had renounced violence and had been great votaries of non-violence. Buddha lived and preached non-violence. In the precepts of the eight-fold path propagated by him, non-violence was the cardinal tenet. Buddha's message was adopted as the state policy by Emperor Ashoka in the third century B.C. Emperor Ashoka himself turned to non-violence after the Kalinga war in which thousands were killed. Mahavir, a contemporary of Gautam Buddha and propagator of Jainism, was the exponent of non-violance which embraced all living creatures. The poet saints of the Bhakti Cult, down to Mahatma Gandhi were all practitioners of non-violence.

The greatest apostle of non-violence in the twentieth century was Mahatma Gandhi, who has gone down in the history of our country as the Father of the Nation. Gandhiji himself did not disapprove the use of violence in certain extreme conditions. He wrote: "I would rather have India resort to arms in order to defend her honour than that she should in a cowardly manner become or remain a helpless victim of her own dishonour". While Gandhiji believed that non-violence is infinitely superior to violence, he would have preferred violence to cowardice if that was the choice before him. "I shall risk violence a thousand times rather than risk the emasculation of a whole race."

It is also relevant that Gandhiji's concept of Ahimsa or non-violence was far wider than mere abstention from physical violence; it embraced avoidance of injury to others in any form. This study will show that the cause of physical violence is often the injustice to the poor and the underprivileged, and their exploitation.

Though Gandhiji himself was wedded to non-violence not only in action but also in thought and word, he realised and often regretted that demonstrations and agitations launched by him could not be kept along non-violent lines for long. Even so, the Independence movement would have resulted in much greater blood shed but for the restraining influence and the moral authority that the Mahatma exercised over the country. It was no fault of Gandhiji that the Independence of India was born in blood and not in peace, and that he himself died a martyr at the hands of an assassin.

We, as a people, are as much prone to violence as any other, in spite of the age long strand of non-violence in our cultural and spiritual heritage. In fact, Indian people generally have not accepted non-violence as a firm guide in practical life; nor have they accepted the view that recourse to violence even as a last resort to get justice is wrong. Events preceding the Independence of India demonstrated how little the people of the coutnry believed in non-violence as a practical concept. The Indian youth had by the end of the 19th century lost faith in the moderates. Mere talk of passive and non-violent resistance did not satisfy them. Filled with the burning hatred of foreign rulers, they came to the conclusion that colonial rule should be overthrown by using every type of physical force available to them. The 'Jugantar', a daily published from Calcutta, representing this trend wrote in April, 1906: "After the Police assault on the peaceful Barisal conference, the 30 crores of people inhabiting India must raise their 60 crore hands to stop this course of oppression. Force must be stopped by force".[1]

In 1904, V.D. Sawarkar had organised Abhinav Bharat as a secret society of revolutionaries. After 1905, several newspapers openly, and a few leaders secretly, began to advocate revolutionary terrorism. The era of revolutionary terrorism had then begun. Their activitics mainly took two forms: the assassination of oppressive officers, informers and traitors from their own rank and dacoity to raise funds for purchase of arms. The latter came to be popularly known as 'Swadeshi dacoities'. As a historian put it: 'They (the revolutionaries) gave us back the pride of our manhood".[2]

About 700 incidents of terrorism were officially listed all over the country during the years 1917 to 1936.

It was not *satyagraha* alone that brought freedom to India. While individual and collective non-violent *satyagraha* helped to create and arouse the nation's awareness to the problem, the examples of several revolutionaries and among them, the examples of Bhagat Singh and Chandra Shekhar Azad, fired the imagination of the youth and made them pledge their lives to the cause of the country's freedom.

The exploits of Netaji Subhash Chandra Bose and the Indian National Army created such an impact on the minds of the people of the country that even Jawaharlal Nehru donned the black gown once again, long after he had given up practice at the Bar, to stand up for the defence of the men and women of the Indian National Army at their trial in Red Fort. The contribution to the Independence movement by the naval mutiny was also significant.

Thus there was considerable physical violence accompanying our Independence movement. When a movement is on a national plane and with reference to a cause which affects the entire population, the normal reaction is to condone the accompanying violence in view of the importance and the dimensions of the cause itself. This is turn implies that violence generated is measured against the importance of the cause in so far as it affects the society. Violence both in its quality and quantum is in fact directly related to the intensity of the commitment of the people to the cause. It is not entirely logical and correct, therefore, to view violence only in the context of the largeness or smallness of the cause, but more in the light of the degree of involvement of the people with the cause, whatever that happens to be at the given time. It is not so much the objective importance of the cause that matters; it is the number of people committed to it and the extend to which the furtherance of the cause affects the lives of the people involved.

The simple definition of violence is behaviour designed to inflict injury on a person or damage to property. This definition conceals more than it reveals and explains. In any human society, a physical strike or hurt is understood and accepted as the most obvious expression of violence but this is only one of its several forms or faces. I have already referred to Gandhiji's concept of violence. According to Martin Luther King, depriving a Negro child of decent food and clothing is a severe form of violence. Nearer home, in our own country, treating a section of our population as untouchables and not allowing them to come anywhere near hundred yards of the so-called upper caste, a practice in certain parts of the country until a few years back and which has since disappeared, was one of the cruelest forms of violence, much more humiliating and destructive of human dignity than even physical assault. To people who have been so humiliated over centuries, resort to violence in extreme conditions of harassment is a psychological relief and release, particularly when all their silent sufferings and forebearance had only given then fresh doses of humiliation. Subjecting an individual or a group to patent acts of injustices is another aspect of violence. Exploitation in any form, social or economic, is yet another angle to violence. Treating people in a manner which is contrary to the accepted norms of human dignity too is a form of violence. That the latter categories of victims are not subjected to overt physical injury or even apparent hurt, does not exclude such cases from the concept of violence in its comprehensive sweep. Broadly any act, whether overt or covert, that coerces or causes physical hurt, material loss or mental anguish or which degrades human beings or which militates against human rights, dignity and decency should be viewed as an act of violence. Thus all acts which have anything to do, among others, even with child labour, bonded labour, practice of untouchability and similar acts of discrimination either with regard to groups or communities, fall within the scope of the term of violence. In the process, I have accepted this wider concept of violence, instend of limiting it only to its overt physical manifestations. It is violence in this limited concept which has generally received the attention of many scholars in the field of social sciences, even though the roots of physical violence lie in the organisation and functioning of a society.

My own concept of violence is based on my experience of handling violence in the field, as a police officer for thirty two years. My emphasis therefore, will be more on the socio-economic, political and administrative factors which contribute to and create conditions conducive to physical violence. In this context, an effort will be made to identify some of the important areas and causes of violence in a few of the states.

Before proceeding further, it is necessary to make it clear that the expression 'violence' has been used throughout this study in the context of social violence and not of individual violence. Proneness to violence in individuals can be inherited or acquired by environmental factors. But social violence is largely the product of a socio-economic and/or a political system which is characterised by gross social injustice and exploitation. In such a system, violence can be either due to the deprived and depressed sections trying to assert themselves and acquire their legitimate role and entitlements and/or it can also be due to vested interests trying to hold on to what control they have over the victims of violence for years and refusing to part with this control.

While we routinely condemn violence, we fail to take note of the contributions that each one of us is unconsciously making towards it in our efforts to promote our own vested interests. While we do shun violence as a general principle, we do not fail to take recourse to it if it helps us to realise our selfish aims or goals. Most of us do not hesitate to use violence in one or more of its forms, may not always be in its physical manifestation, in the pursuit of our goals, and we see nothing wrong in the process. At the same time, we would not like to see the other person or group use violence against us. As long as this dichotomy in our perception of violence as applied to "us" and "them" persists, violence will continue to be the ultimate sanction for deciding conflicting interests between unequal segments in a largely exploitative society. Whether this violence is warranted and is desirable or not, will be determined by the context in which it has been used, by whom used, for what ultimate purpose it is used and from whose point of view it is perceived. Therefore, it is necessary to start with the assumption that while violence *per se* is an undesirable and avoidable element in human dealings, its inevitability and function have also to be viewed in the various socio-economic and political contexts in which it is resorted to. Seen in this light, violence may be unavoidable in human affairs, particularly in a society where large segments of the population are the victims of iniquities arising out of gross inequalities and unequal opportunities. Thus considered, violence or even the mere threat of it, if it is credible enough, can well be an agent of social change. Violence may be inevitable, except in an utopian society. Often, violence may be the spur to generate the political will for the creation of a just society.

To quote from John Gunn's 'Violence in Human Society': "Violence has biological and social functions, important to our evolution. Its total elimination, therefore, will leave a hiatus; Unless that can be filled by an equally powerful evolutionary force, it is possible that man will be worse, not better off. Perhaps all we need to do is to ensure that, while violence may continue, destructiveness does not get out of hand so that we can avoid the ultimate cataclysm."[3] This calls for the instruments of the state which have to deal with violence to be maintained in a proper state of functional competence. This has special relevance to the Criminal Justice System of which the police and the judiciary are the two major of the three components, the third being the jails.

The failure of the Indian state and its instruments to cope with the problems arising in the process of socio-economic change in a society with adult suffrage and equality of opportunity and status, among other similar objectives provided in our Constitution, has led to rising expectations on the one hand, and growing consciousness of the exploitation and indignity in social relations, on the other. Such a combination has inevitably led to strong resentment expressing itself in physical violence.

Policies are proclaimed and promises made which remain unfulfilled. Laws are enacted which are not fairly and effectively implemented because of strong vested interests combined with the weak political will and inadequacies of the adminstration.

Unless these infirmities are removed and progress made towards the creation of a truly just and non-exploitative social order, violence is not only likely to continue but may get aggravated. With tremendous growth of population, problems have become more acute.

Sean Mac Bride, a Member of the Irish Republican Army in the 1920s and 1930s and winner of the Nobel Prize observed in the course of his Nobel Prize acceptance speech: "If those vested with authority and power practice injustice, resort to torture and killing, is it not inevitable that those who are victims will resort to similar methods?

This does not condone the savagery or inhuman conduct, but does provide a part of the explanation for the increasing violence." Thus viewed, a state which seeks to abjure violence has to ensure a society based on equality of opportunity, equity and justice and the state itself should play the role of an impartial and neutral umpire between conflicting groups and communities, regions and states. If the state can be faulted to whatever degree, whether big or small, it is the state itself that is to blame, if, as a result of its actions or failure to act, there is violence from individuals or groups, regions or states for any wrong or injustice done to them.

This is the basic proposition. If the institutions which already exist are capable of preventing this conflict from escalating into manifest physical violence, to that extent social changes can be expected to be peaceful. If, however the rising tide of change breaks down the control mechanisms and there are no new ones replacing the old to take effective charge of the fall-out from the changes, the society will have to face the consequent violence. Whether this violence will be below the threshold level or whether it will cascade in its intensity and frequency to a level which would imperil the democratic structure that we have given ourselves, will depend entirely on effective and efficient political management of the changes through existing administrative institutions or if necessary, through new ones designed to bring them in tune with the new demands. If the state's response to violence accompanying change is in the form of repression as a substitute for efficient political management as the agent of change, instead of solving the problem, it will only drive it underground and therefore exacerbate it.

An unjust social order produces an environment which fosters and nourishes various forms of violence. If the state fails to redress such an unjust social order, to that extent it forteits its legitimacy in the eyes of the people who are its victims. The process of change that has been inaugurated in India promises to be long and arduous.

The extent to which we are able to anticipate and provide the institutional infrastructural needs in the context of the velocity of change, as also the contents of change, will decide whether we would be able to control violence consequent on the socio-economic change or whether violence will control us. This is the central theme of this study.

References

1. The Telegraph—A national daily published from Calcutta Dt. 12th July, 1985.
2. IBID
3. John Gunnn : "Violence in Human Society" (1973).

PART II
CHAPTER 2

SOCIAL INHERITANCE AT INDEPENDENCE

Bob Jessop makes the point: "that social order is compatible with social change. Indeed the stability of social order may well depend on reorganization of established institutions and also on institutionlised innovations. Social order is possible only through the regulation of interaction between individuals and groups to prevent unlimited struggle and to confine conflicts to institutionalised modes of resolution."[1]

Article 15 of the Constitution of India mentions Right to Equality as a Fundamental Right:

"Article 15(2): No citizen shall, on grounds only of religion, race, caste, sex, place of birth or any of them, be subject to any disability, liability, restriction or condition with regard to—

(a) access to shops, public restaurants, hotels and places of public entertainment; or

(b) the use of well, tanks, bathing ghats, roads and places of public resort maintained wholly or partly out of State funds or dedicated to the use of the general public."

After Independence we have introduced several socio-economic reforms. One of the most important of these which will eventually have the greatest impact on the structure of the Indian society is the law which seeks to remove untouchability by making the practice of it a penal offence. Hitherto the effect of this measure has been merely to loosen and unsettle a structural arrangement which had been legitimised by custom and centuries of accepted practice. In pre-Independent India, the social arrangement on the basis of caste had come to be accepted and acted upon by all sections of the population without any apparent demur, in spite of the several iniquities militating against human respect and dignity inherent in the system. This system had entrenched itself so deeply into the minds of the people that every child, from the time he or she was able to think was influenced and oriented to the system which became integral to his or her mental growth and development. A system so deeply rooted and embedded in the psyche of the people at all levels, which included the deprived as much as the privileged, advantaged as much as the disadvantaged, was being sought to be erased overnight by legislative processes in the wake of the Independence of India. Now the measures introduced to change the system are gradually beginning to yield results. To expect, however, that this change would be sudden or that it would be in the form of a clear cut break with the past or that the transition would be smooth and without the birth pangs of a new society struggling to be born is to underestimate human reactions and resistance to change.

The perniciousness of the caste system as it came to be practised in its most degrading form is the largest single act of social injustice for which our country with all its vaunted philosophical and spiritual heritage, had been justifiably indicted at the bar of world opinion. Whether intended by the original founders of the system or not, the practitioners of the caste system in its most blatant form denied almost the entire range of human rights to the castes at the bottom of the hierarchy. These unfortunate ones were indeed born with a human face but were, as if, scooped hollow of all their human emotions. It would appear that even their right to feeling had not been recognised. Except for their face, there was very little in terms of human attributes and rights that they were entitled to in their dealings with the society in which they were born, in which they survived and from which eventually made their exit. Society dealt with them as so many faceless and nameless beings using them almost as consumer durables and expendable in the extreme. They had no relevance to themselves, much less to the lives they led. Their relevance was only in relation to the role that the society had determined for them, which they were expected to fulfil from the beginning to the end with no choice whatever of their own or in inter-personal relationships. They were as much as owned by the members of the dominant castes in society and were left with nothing which they could call their own. Even their wives and daughters had in some cases to wait on the pleasures of the dominant caste members who owned them and provided the only *raison d'etre* for their continued survival, in whatever conditions were decided for them. Abraham Joshua Heschel wrote: "There is a form of oppression which is more painful and scathing than physical injury or economic privation. It is public humiliation."[2]

Next to slavery in its most abject form, here was a dispensation which packed into the system so much of latent violence. In such a situation, the mere threat of violence was so convincingly credible that it had seldom to be put to test. This violence of iniquity, violence of exploitation and violence of denial of human rights, is an important part of the concept of violence and is as much condemnable as physical violence which, however, forms the central theme in most studies of violence. That these categories of violence were practised as a matter of course and remained concealed without any tangible or dramatic impact in the society does not mitigate its heinousness and viciousness or the damge it did to the human personality. "No matter what psychic armour we wear, none of us is immune to the message we receive from others about our own worth. And the primary message lower class people receive about themselves is that they have no worth—that they are irrelevant or expendable, if indeed they exist at all."[3]

B.R. Ambedkar, moving the final reading of the Constitution in the Constituent Assembly of India on November 29, 1949, observed: "On the secial plane we have in India a society based on the principles of graded inequality which means elevation of some and degradation for others. On the economic plane, we have some who have immense wealth as against many who live in abject poverty. On 26th January, 1950 we are going to enter into a life of contradiction. In politics, we will have equality and in social and economic life we will have inequality. We must remove this contradiction at the earliest possible moment or else, those who suffer from inequality will blow up the structure of political democracy which this Assembly has so laboriously built up."

We are still in the process of dismantling what we had inherited and are seeking to replace the system with one based on equality and adult suffrage. We have set ourselves the task of ushering in a society in which violence of injustice, violence to human dignity, and violence to human rights will all become a part of history that we have left behind. For too long we have had a society which can aptly be described in the words of Rabindranath Tagore as one in which 'the few are more than the many', though Tagore himself had used these words in the context of the unequal world.

Even now, more than three decades after making untouchability a penal offence, there are several States in the country where this sinister practice has survived, though in a diluted and concealed form. There is considerable gap even now between the intention of the Constitutional abolition of untouchability wiht a law to punish it, and what actually obtains on the ground.

I discussed with M.N. Shrniwas, the noted Indian

Sociologist, the subject of untouchability as practised in Karnataka. According to him, the society in Karnataka has arrived at an unspoken arrangement between the Scheduled Castes and the upper castes. He refers to this "as a separate but unequal arrangement" While all the needs of the Scheduled Castes are met, they do not come into open conflict with the caste susceptibilities of the upper castes. This in effect means a continued observance of untouchability by both parties without making it appear to be so. Though there are occasional complaints by the Scheduled Castes against the upper castes, these complaints are seldom followed to their logical conclusion in the courts of law in accordance with the statute.

The Indian caste system institutionalised an arrangement which automatically gave the upper castes a place in society to which the lower castes could never aspire, let alone arrive at. In a sense this ensured that those who were at the lower level in the hierarchy of castes remained condemned to their social and economic existence on the basis of social disabilities and the economic deprivation which were part of the system. This arrangement remained self-fulfilling since there was hardly any organized effort to disturb the system over the centuries for reasons which were peculiar to and characteristic of the successive rulers. The result was that the Scheduled Castes, and to a lesser extent the backward communities not only remained without any means to propel themselves forward to a higher level of social and economic existence, but they also did not have the motivation to do so in as much as they took it for granted that there was no place for them above a certain level which had been determined generations before them by man and history. There was no point for them in aspiring for any upward social mobility.

It was this mental attitude of acceptance of the inherited state of affairs which was for the first time being sought to be changed by several social reformatory steps that were taken in the years immediatel following

Independence. Thus when the Harijans and the Adivasis aspire for a higher position in life which had been denied them over centuries, the upper castes feel their social status, economic opportunities and political power threatened from below. The strains in the rural as well as the urban set up and the violence that spills over occasionally are all the birth pangs of the transformation that is being witnessed in different communities constituting the nation. "All modern societies have to resolve the tensions between the ideal and the realities, but the tradition is most glaring and extreme in Indian society......... It is only when things are changing that worst brutalities take place, especially where any attempt is made to improve the conditions of Scheduled Castes."[4]. Even so, what is being attempted now is merely the equal treatment of unequals. We are yet far from the constitutionally stipulated goal of equality in its various forms.

It would be simplistic to pretend that the concept of equality, merely by being enshrined in our Constitution would provide the ultimate solution to the problems of economic and social inequality. We are living in a society where the hiatus between the rights enjoyed by the poor and those by the privileged is far too wide for an increasingly conscious people, politically aware of their rights to continue to tolerate the present system. They do now articulate their demands as they have never done before, and what is more can disrupt the delicate structure of democracy by organising themselves into so many pressure groups. They are so very vital to the integrity of the system that they cannot be ignored. Poverty in its most distressing sense is not mere want. It is want without the hope of a foreseeably better future.

References

1. Bob Jessop: "Social Order, Reform and Revolution" (1972).
2. Abraham Joshua Heschel quoted by Charles E. Silberman in "Criminal Violence and Criminal Justice" (1978).

3. Charles E. Silberman : "Criminal Violence and Criminal Justice" (1978).
4. Andre Beteille's interview, The Hindu, a national daily Dt. 6th April, 1980.

CHAPTER 3

SOCIO-ECONOMIC CHANGE AMONG SCHEDULED CASTES AND SCHEDULED TRIBES. THEIR EDUCATION AND EMPLOYMENT PROFILE

Two factors which have considerably contributed to violence in the country in the past years have been communalism and socio-economic change arising from the upward mobility of the Scheduled Castes, Scheduled Tribes and the other weaker sections through several programmes initiated by the Government. I have dealt with communalism in a separate book. There are certain important aspects of Scheduled Castes and Scheduled tribes, which should first be mentioned in broad terms. These are: the Scheduled Castes suffer not only from economic exploitation but from social discrimination. Their poverty is appalling and they have very little by way of assets. The bulk of them depend on agricultural wages for their livelihood, (Annexure A and B). 48.2% and 32.7% of the agricultural workers in India are drawn from Scheduled Castes and Scheduled Tribes (Annexure C). 28.2% of the Scheduled Castes are cultivators, mostly small and marginal farmers, share-croppers and tenants. Annexure C1 gives information on the percentage of Scheduled Castes and Scheduled Tribes to the total agricultural labour in different states along with the percentage of land allotted to them. Annexure at C2 gives the total area of land allotted to Scheduled Castes and Scheduled Tribes, state-wise. Considering the volume of violence to which the Scheduled Castes who work as share-croppers are subjected, the report of the Working Group of the Development of Scheduled Castes had recommended in 1980 the conferment of legal rights of occupancy and purchase of ownership on easy terms as two of the most important steps in the economic development of the Scheduled Castes. Even the land allotted to them has not been in their actual control in some of the states. There is awareness at the Government level about the nexus between the economic deprivation and the social discrimination of the Scheduled Castes and the atrocities that continue to be committed on them by the dominant castes. According to a recent national survey, the Scheduled Castes form 66% of the estimated number of Bonded labourers while the Scheduled Tribes constitute an additional 18%.

The statement at Annexure D gives an idea of some notorious cases of atrocities on Harijans Though the police is expected under the provision of the Protection of Civil Rights Act to prosecute all those who discriminate against the Scheduled Castes, the actual impact of this Act has been nominal. In the course of prosecution, they face several constraints, most of which they are not able to overcome. One of the major difficulties is that the complainants themselves as well as the witnesses do not want to pursue these cases in courts for fear of reprisals, as they still have to live in the same village with those who discriminate against them. The statement at Annexure E gives an idea about the percentage of acquittals of cases under the Protection of Civil Rights Act in the courts. Out of all the cases registered by the police, only between 55 and 60% are prosecuted in courts. Out of the cases thus prosecuted as many as 89% ended in acquittal in 1982. This speaks amply of the utter ineffectiveness of the prosecutions prescribed for curing society of this grave social malady. Statements at E1 and E2 give the State-wise picture of the cases under the Protection of Civil Rights Act, 1956.

Interestingly, the social evil of untouchability is not as much in evidence in West Bengal and the eastern states compared to other states. Admittedly the only yardstick for measuring this evil is the number of cases registered under the Protection of Civil Rights Act. At best this is a crude tool of measurement since for various reasons, many of the cases reported at the Police Stations are not registered by the Police.

Statements at E3 and E4 give state-wise number of cases of atrocities committed on the Scheduled Castes and Scheduled Tribes. 'Atrocity' is not a legal terminology. However, crimes committed against Scheduled Castes and Scheduled Tribes by others are generally referred to as atrocities.

The figures of atrocities on Scheduled Castes and Scheduled Tribes are available upto 1982. The data shows an upward trend in certain states from 1980 onwards. The highest number of atrocities was registered in Madhya Pradesh during 1982, followed by Uttar Pradesh, Bihar and Rajasthan. An analysis of the motives behind the cases of atrocity against the Scheduled Castes and Scheduled Tribes was made by the Commission for Scheduled Castes and Scheduled Tribes. The Commission came to the conclusion that in 32% of the cases, the motives could not be ascertained. Of the remaining 68% of the cases, the largest single cause was land dispute which accounted for 16% of the cases. In many cases allotment of surplus land to the landless poor was the cause of trouble. The Commission recommended that actual handing over of the physical possession of surplus land to the allottee must be ensured even if it would entail an amendment of the existing law. Next to land dispute, denial of minimum wages accounted for 12% of the cases. Demand for minimum wages, as fixed by the Government and refusal by the land owners to pay according to the prescribed rates have been responsible for creating many situations even resulting in murders.

Increasing number of crimes by the other caste groups againt the Scheduled Castes and Scheduled Tribes is in no small measure due to the delay in the investigation of cases and the poor rate of conviction of the accused persons. The Commission in its second report for the period ending March, 1980 observed: "A review of convictions and acquittals ratio of cases of atrocities against the Scheduled Castes and Scheduled tribes in Gujarat from where complete data was received reveals that the percentage of conviction to the total decided cases for Scheduled Castes comes to 10.8% and in case of Scheduled Tribes it is 10.6%. This is an exceedingly low percentage.............. 95.45% and 91.41% is the acquittal rate in the case of murders against the Scheduled Castes and Scheduled tribes respectively." The same pattern with very slight variations is seen in most of the other states where the Scheduled Castes and the Scheduled Tribes are victims of atrocities. Unless this trend is reversed through institutional innovations in the prevailing Criminal Justice System, the relief to victims through criminal prosecution of the offenders would continue to be insignificant.

In Uttar Pradesh and Bihar there is a system of setting up Harijan Police Stations. These Police Stations are intended exclusively to register all cases of atrocities against Harijans, regardless of jurisdictional constraints and geographical location of the homes of complainants. One wonders whether this is a correct approach to a problem so very widespread in these States. By registering complaints at Police Stations located outside the jurisdiction of the complainant's Police Station, the investigations of the cases are rendered more difficult than necessary. As most of the complaints have the potential of developing into serious law and order problems, it is inadvisable to keep the concerned police stations out of the picture initially as it dilutes their responsibility for prevention and detection of such outrages.

In a letter addressed on March 12, 1980 to all the Chief Ministers and Governors Smt. Indira Gandhi observed : "There is a clear nexus between economic plight of the Scheduled Castes and the atrocities and social disabilities to which they are subjected. Many of these crimes are intended to terrorise and cow down the Scheduled

Castes when they seek their wages for agricultural labour or try to cultivate the land legally allotted to them. A permanent solution to this situation must be based on the rapid economic development of the Scheduled Castes." This shows awareness at official levels especially at Prime Minister's level to the resistance that the vested interests have been offering to the upward economic mobility of the Scheduled Castes.

The literacy rate of the Scheduled Castes and the Scheduled Tribes for the whole country for the years 1931, 1961, 1971 and 1981 may be seen at Annexure F1. It was not possible to get information on this for 1951. It would be evident that there has been a distinct improvement in the level of education of these two weaker sections. The statewise figures of literacy among the Scheduled Castes and Scheduled Tribes in 1961, 1971 and 1981 may be seen in Annexure F2, F and G.

According to the report of the Commissioner for Scheduled Castes and Scheduled Tribes for the period 1979 to 1981, the educational programmes for the Scheduled Castes and the Scheduled Tribes have not had the desired impact. According to 1981 Census, literacy rate among the Scheduled Castes was 21.38%. This was composed of 31.12% males and 10.98% females. The corresponding figures for the general population exclusive of Scheduled Castes and Scheduled tribes was 41.30% which was composed of 52.34% males and 29.42% females. In Bihar, Haryana, Madhya Pradesh, Orissa, Punjab, Uttar Pradesh and West Bengal, the female illiteracy among the Scheduled Castes and Scheduled Tribes was over 90%. According to the Education Ministry's 1981 resport, Karnataka had more than 50% of non-enrolled boys in the age group of 6 to 11 i.e. at the primary school level from the Scheduled castes and scheduled tribes. Similarly, figures for girls from Scheduled Castes and Scheduled Tribes in this age group in some of the states were Bihar 79%, Haryana 73%, Karnataka 58% and Uttar Pradesh 74%.

Another indicator of their educational backwardness is the high rate of drop-out. The report of the Commissioner for Scheduled Castes and Scheduled Tribes 1979-1981, revealed that these rates at the primary school stage were 74% in Bihar, 77% in Karnataka; 74% in Uttar Pradesh and 80% in Madhya Pradesh.

Though the all India percentage of literacy among the Scheduled Castes and the Scheduled Tribes stood at 21.38 and 16.35 according to the 1981 Census, the Scheduled Castes have done educationally much better in Gujarat, Maharashtra and Kerala. A table giving the literacy rates of the Scheduled Castes and the Scheduled Tribes in the states may be seen in Annexure F and G. The distinct improvement registered by the Scheduled Castes in Gujarat, Maharashtra and Kerala compared to the Scheduled Castes of Bihar and Uttar Pradesh between 1971 and 1981 should explain to some extent the greater awareness and self-assertion which characterise the Scheduled Castes in those states compared to the Scheduled castes in Bihar and Uttar Pradesh. The improvement registered by the Scheduled Tribes in the field of education in Gujarat and Maharashtra has not been to the same extent as by the Scheduled Castes although the literacy rates among the Scheduled Tribes in Gujarat and Maharashtra are distinctly higher than those in Bihar.

The number of post-matric scholarships awarded to the Scheduled Castes and Scheduled Tribes students show an extremely steep rise in 1981-82compared to 1951-1952. In terms of public expenditure involved, the increase in higher still as shown at Annexure H.

In the case of scholarships paid to the Scheduled Castes and Scheduled Tribes a 'means test' has been laid down. According to this, students whose parents/ guardians' income from all sources does not exceed Rs. 750/- per month will get full fees waiver. Students whose parents'/ guardians' income from all sources exceeds Rs. 750/- per month but does not exceed Rs. 1,000/- per month and who pursue professional studies such as Medical, Engineering and B.Sc. Agriculture, get full maintenance allowance and full fees waiver. Students who pursue diploma courses in Medicine and Engineering get half maintenance allowance and waiver of full fees. Students whose parents'/guardians' income from all sources exceeds Rs. 1,000/-per month get no scholarship. One unique feature of the scheme is that all eligible Scheduled Caste/Scheduled Tribes students are awarded scholarships and their number is not predetermined nor limited by allocated funds. Though the scheme is centrally sponsored, it is operated through the State Governments.

Unless the authorities ensure that these scholarship holders use the money for the purpose for which it is intended, the effort for the educational improvement of the weaker sections may be substantially defeated. I was told that in Bihar the Tribals who avail of the scholarships do not pursue their studies diligently. Their link with the educational institutions is limited to collecting the monthly scholarships. Inspite of such aberrations, it is heartening to note that the Scheduled castes and the Scheduled Tribes have registered a distinct improvement in terms of educational qualifications of all categories as will be evident from the numbers of educated job seekers on the registers of employment exchanges in some of the selected states. While one does feel encourgaged by the improvement that these categories are showing, considered in absolute terms, they still have considerable leeway to make up. The statements at Annexures I and J give the position of Scheduled Castes and scheduled Tribes enrolments in the Universities at the graduate and post-graduate levels between 1977 and 1979. The percentages quoted in these two statements give the relative position of these two groups in the total enrolments in the Universities. The growth achieved by these communities during the period between 1977 and 1979 though only marginal, is still significant. The tables at Annexures K, K1 and K2 give the progressive total of the unemployed (both educated and uneducated) in the live registers of the employment exchanges during 1978, 1984 and 1985. The percentage component of the Scheduled Caste, in the total educated figuring in the live register of the Employment Exchanges for the period ending 1980 is shown in Annexure L.

The statements at Annexure M and N give information on the increase registered by the Scheduled Cates and the Scheduled Tribes in the live registers of the Employment Exchanges during 1980 to 1984 in all the faculties including the professional fields. Even between the period 1980 and 1984, one can see the increase registered in courses such as Commerce, Engineering, Medical and Science, particularly in the States of Uttar Pradesh, Maharashtra, Gujarat, Karnataka and Bihar. This would give an idea of the trend that is discernible among the Scheduled Castes and Scheduled Tribes in terms of demand for employment opportunities. The position with regard to the Scheduled Tribes is that their performance has been poor compared to Scheduled Castes as may be seen from Annexure N.

Annexure O gives the progress in the percentage of the Scheduled Castes and Scheduled Tribes employees under the Central Gvoernment in the various categories between 1970 and 1980. Considering the increase in the number of professional candidates under both these categories between 1980 and 1984 in some of the states (Annexure M and N) it is to be expected that the employment figures in the various Class I, Class II and Class III services will record a much steeper and more rapid increase in 1990 compared to 1980, in turn compared to 1970.

According to the 34th Report of the Union Public Service Commission (UPSC) for the period April 1, 1983 to March 31, 1984, candidates belonging to Scheduled Castes and Scheduled Tribes continued to be recommended for employment by the Commission by relaxed criteria, provided they were considered fit for appointment to the particular posts. The Commission was able to recommend candidates belonging to Scheduled Castes against all the vacancies reserved for them in the examination requiring general academic qualifications such as a degree of a recognised University or equivalent as in the case of the Civil Services Examination, 1982; Indian Economic Services Examination, 1983 and Assistants' Grade Examination, 1982. In other examinations including those requiring technical or professional qualifications the performance of Scheduled Castes candidates had been satisfactory and the Commission was able to meet fully the reserved quota for Scheduled Castes candidates in the case of the combined Medical Service examination, 1983 (Annexure Q). In respect of the engineering Services Examination, 1982, Indian Forest Service Examination 1983 and Stenographers' examination 1983 even though the Commission could not meet the quota fully, the performance of the Scheduled Castes candidates had shown an improvement over the previous years. In the case of the Scheduled Tribe candidates also, the Commission recommended candidates for all vacancies reserved for them in the examinations requiring technical or professional qualifications. Candidates to the full extent of reservation could be recommended in the case of the combined Medical Services Examination only in 1982 and 1983, but not in earlier years. The performance of the Scheduled Tribes in the Engineering Services examination, 1982 was on the whole better even though the Commission could not recommend the required number of candidates to fill up all the vacancies reserved for them.

The UPSC figures of selection for the period 1968 to 1972 may be seen at Annexure P. It was not possible to get the figures for the period earlier to this. The only significant comparison between Annexure 'P' and 'Q' is the increase registered in the number of Scheduled Castes and Scheduled tribes candidates who had appeared in the examinations for recruitment to the Engineering Services.

This shows a distinct increase in the period 1979 to 1983 in the number of candidates who appeared at the examinations though the number of candidates who qualified themselves and were recommended for employment continues to be very much lower than the quota for Scheduled Tribes. In this regard, the Scheduled Castes have improved distinctly in 1979-1983 over their performance in 1968-1972.

It will be seen from Annexure P and Q that in a few services there were more Scheduled Castes and Tribes candidates than the decided quota. If they are unable to compete with the open market candidates for selection in other jobs, they may feel resentful and swell the ranks of angry young men. In the very process of increasing the educational capability of the Scheduled Castes and Scheduled Tribes, by not being able to offer them worthwhile jobs, an additional factor contributing to social tension and eventual violence would be created. In this class of candidates who have been left out there may be quite a number who may be the first generation applicants seeking the benefit of the reserved quota and who may have been edged out by candidates from the same category but were economically stronger and whose families may have availed of the reservation for one or even two generations. With the stronger among the weaker snatching the reservation advantages in successive generations, it is possible to visualise a stage when those who have not had any benefit of the reservation even though qualified, may agitate for modification of the reservation concept to provide for 'descheduling' those Scheduled Castes and Scheduled Tribes who have availed of the first and even second generation benefits.

Statistics of growth in any field of human activity does not reflect intangible and unmeasurable factors such as sense of justice, self-respect, dignity, equity and the like which should also result from educational and economic betterment. These components are different in the attitude and character between one person and another. The frustration and anger of an educated unemployed youth can be far more destructive than that of an uneducated one. When such frustration builds up over a period of time, one can sense and almost smell violence in the air. Unemployment will be the most over-arching issue in the coming years, putting in the shade the other problems. The reservation policy will then have to be reviewed even if it may be only to ensure that the benefit of the reservation is so spread out as to benefit as many of the families of the weaker sections as possible.

According to a report in the Illustrated Weekly of India, November 30, 1986 by Nikhil Lakshman[1], the state of unemployment in the country, even in 1986 was quite alarming. The Beggar Home in Bangalore had two graduates and two post-graduates as members. "When the Kerala Govt. conducted its competitive examination for 100 clerical jobs, 45,000 candidates applied. Tamil Nadu had 45,531 professionals registered, including 2414 doctors and 2030 engineers in the Employment Exchanges. West Bengal's Minister of State for Labour told the State Assembly that 2000 doctors and 1490 engineers were unemployed. In Bihar, a group of unemployed civil engineers descended in the heart of Patna with begging bowls and carrying placards that read 'We are unemployed. Give us alms". It is only a short step from begging to banditry. Unemployment figures are in Annexures K, K1 and K2.

The incidence of social conflicts in different parts of rural India since the seventies has been more pronounced than in first two decades after independence. To an extent, this can be explained. In the years immediately following Independence, though there were legislative enactments and verbal assurances about the intended changes in the social and economic system of the country, for various reasons, implementation was extremely limited. The land reforms took their own time to become effective and even now their implementation is halting and evasive. During the earlier years, the Scheduled Castes, Scheduled Tribes and the weaker sections continued to be in the same state of mental torpor as they had been over the centuries and were yet to grasp the value of their newly conferred rights and entitlements. This suited the upper castes and in the absence of an assertive demand for the enjoyment of the acquired mobility in their social and economic status, the upper castes were pleased to let them wallow in the same state in which they had been for centuries. But as years passed and the impact of the land reforms, the Removal of the Untouchability Act and the reservation policy was felt, larger segments of the disadvantaged became aware that a qualitatively better life awaited them if only they would bestir themselves to reach out to what were their legitimate dues. It is this awakening of what had been denied to them, and an understanding that this condition was not necessarily inevitable that converted a supine acceptance into an active and exploitable grievance. Almost from the beginning of the seventies, with the awareness among the weaker sections increasing, conflicts consequent on the social change became more strident. Nobody parts with power, wealth and privileges willingly. This results in inevitable conflict and this is what has been in evidence in the rural sector in the seventies and eighties. The very idea of having to respond to a demand from the weaker sections who until recently had accepted whatever was thrown at, and to them condescendingly was taken as an indignity by certain sections of the upper castes who over the centuries never had the experience of responding to any demands posed by Scheduled Castes and Scheduled Tribes. The question of demands from these groups just did not arise.

M.N. Srinivas in his paper on 'Living in a Revolution'[2] has pointed out how the traditional caste hierarchy in the country has resulted in a particular ethos of social relationship between the people pursuing different trades and operations. With the abolition of untouchability in law if not completely in fact, and the provisions made by the Government in service and in education, this ethos has undergone considerable change. The Scheduled Castes who earlier were always at the receiving end of patronage from the upper castes, found that the position has been partially reversed by the democratic process by which they had come to occupy positions from where they were in a position to dispense favours to the upper castes. Many members belonging to the upper castes had now to approach ministers, legislators and high Government functionaries belonging to the Scheduled Castes and Scheduled Tribes for help and support. This is a reversal of roles which occured for the first time in the history of our country. This is one of the most significant social changes that has been achieved by the country through democratic process alone. We are witnesses to the impact of this in the Indian society.

This change is certainly whetting the appetite of large segments among the weaker sections who have not yet had their share of things. This in turn will naturally breed a degree of frustration and even violence because open display of defiance of the high caste dominance by the educated youth among the Scheduled Castes and Scheduled Tribes is becoming a common phenomenon. This trend is likely to become more pronounced in the years to come as the numerical strength of the provileged among the weaker sections increases as also their level of education, and with it their sense of awareness.

The changes that have been brought about demand a new pattern of inter-personal human relationship which require a measure of adaptability of the participants which has not been forthcoming to the extent requried in some regions and in some states. This too has given rise to conflicts and consequent violence which appear to be the concomitant of the ongoing social change. So long as a society remains relatively stable and unchanging, the problems generated in the society are of a routine and predictable nature. As society changes, and in the absence of adequate preparation and without a gestation period for absorption of the effects of change by the groups and communities concerned, the fall-out from the changes often includes violence. This has happened in the states in the Hindi-belt. The intensity and the frequency of violence in the states of Bihar and Uttar Pradesh should be attributed to the social changes that have come about during the last two decades. The social change in the Southern states has been spread over a longer time frame with much less manifest violence, thought the reluctance and unwillingness for adjustment on the part of the vested interests has been the same.

The process of improving the status of the Scheduled Castes and backward castes had started in the South much before India attained Independence. In what was then known as Mysore State, a committee known as the Miller Committee had gone into the conditions of living and other aspects of life of the backward communities in the early twenties. This Committee had come up with recommendations for mitigating the hardships and ameliorating their conditions. The backward class movement had also figured prominently in the then Madras Presidency which comprised much of the area in the states of Andhra Pradesh, Tamil Nadu and Kerala. As far back as 1926 the Government of Madras Presidency had issued a communal G.O. (Government Order) extending facilities for jobs and education to the backward communities. Narayana Guru had launched the reformist movement in the Travancore State of the present day Kerala even in the latter half of the 19th century. Thus the Southern States have had a much earlier start in implementing socio-economic reforms for the uplift of the backward communities. Even though spread over several decades the change that has come about has only blunted to some extent the sharpness of the caste divide in the South. Much of it still exists though in a rather subdued form. The conversion of hundreds of Harijan families to Islam in

Meenakshipuram in Tamil Nadu a few years back is a pointer to the continued presence of ostracism that the Scheduled Castes still have to suffer at the hands of other castes. In the Meenakshipuram case the conversion was a protest by the Harijans against the atrocities of the intermediate castes who themselves until a few decades back were at the receiving end of the indignities meted out to them by the upper castes. They conveniently forgot that what they are doing today to the Harijans was what was done to them by the upper castes until the other day. Their socio-economic upward mobility has given them a status and power and with it an aggressiveness which is difficult to explain. There is something common between the North and the South in this context. In the States of Uttar Pradesh and Bihar some of the atrocities on the Harijans today are committed as much by the intermediate castes who have stood to gain more than anyone else because of the land reforms and other ameliorative measures since Independence.

The point however, that needs to be made is that the number of incidents of atrocities against Harijans culminating in violence is much lower in the Southern states than in the North though it is still present. The number of official posts occupied by persons from the backward communities in the South is particularly high and in the States of Karnataka and Tamil Nadu it is as high as about 70%. All these factors have certainly blurred the caste divide even if it has not completely eliminated it.

References

1. NIKHIL LAKSHMAN : "Despair, Frustration and Anger" Illustrated weekly of India, 30th November, 1986.
2. M.N. Srinivas—A paper: "Living in a Revolution' (1985)

Note: Throughout this study 'Harijans' and 'Scheduled Castes' have been used as interchangable terms. This has been the practice now for decades.

CHAPTER 4

INFRASTRUCTURAL INFIRMITIES

While accepting the fact of change, and even to some extent the fall-out of violence which will have to be treated as a concomitant of change, we would be in a position to control and limit it, if only we have the necessary institutional infrastructure designed for this porpose. Our old institutions have grown decrepit, obsolete to such an extent that they are incapable of coping with the variety of problems in their new virulence. The situation has been compounded by the absence of institutions for handling the first time problems never encountered before, presenting new challenges. Some of the problems leading to violence are: non-payment of minimum wages, land tenurial uncertainty, unfavourable terms for share croppers, continuance of bonded and child labour even after legislation abolishing them, exploitation of tribals, consequences of vast developmental programmes, intercaste tensions, elections to local bodies and legislatures on the basis of adult franchise and the trail of bitterness that follows the elections in certain states. Though several institutions have come up in the country in the context of the developmental plans, considering the peculiarities, special characteristics and the seriousness of the problems thrown up by various new issues, it is imperative that special institutional safeguards are made available close to the areas of their origin to contain them from aggravating into avoidable violence. Instead, what has been attempted is a mere patchwork of the inherited institutions. Many of the issues which eventually erupted into violence, and often violence of a very serious nature in Bihar and Uttar Pradesh initially came to the notice of Government agencies only through routine reports of complaints, which were casually treated by the police as coming under non-cognizable provisions of law. Complaints arising out of conflicts between different castes, or conflicts between tribals and non-tribals, or conflicts related to agrarian problems such as tenurial rights, or the payment of minimum wages, would not in their incipient stages come under the category of cognizable offences under the law. If there was a provision under the law, or something in the nature of an administrative arrangement capable of taking charge of these types of problems at their incipient stages and action was taken to resolve them before they led to heightened bitterness and hostility, many of the issues which eventually erupted into multiple murders could well have been averted. Even the institutions that exist at present are not used purposefully and promptly, because of extraneous considerations.

Laws, regulations and powers of agencies of enforcement, as conceived under the British regime, were designed to meet requirements different from those of post-Independent India. Under imperial rule, there had to be necessarily a docile acceptance of authority. The Indian society was strongly structured and social and economic relations were largely stable and static. With some cosmetic changes, we are still continuing with the same institutional framework of legal and administrative safeguards, though conditions have changed radically. The ethos, psychology and values of a free people are substantially different from those of a subjugated population. In terms of peace and order, it has been a costly omission not to make fundamental changes in laws, and to reformulate the powers and functions of governmental agencies, in order to control and prevent violence which is incidental to social change. It has also to be recognized that the higher levels of administrators under the British rule could function with greater independence and impartiality, circumscribed only by larger imperial interests. They were not subject to the kind of political, communal, caste, and other extraneous pressures that have been plaguing the administration in recent years. Foreign rule had to prove itself by maintaining peace and order, and by apparently fair dealings; foreign rule would have been even less tolerable if the administration under it were not effective, and impartial between one group and another or one individual and another. This compulsion to appear fair in order to continue to rule seems to have disappeared at least partly with the advent of self-rule.

In terms of attitude, training, composition and even deployment, the police need to be totally redesigned to meet the demands made on it by the number of new problems which are the by-products of some of the social reforms and programmes of the Government in the post-Independence period. The Indian police, as an institution is left woefully out of tune with the requirements of the changed scenario, forgetting that the police constitute the vital instrument in the hands of the government for controlling and preventing violence. Failure to up-date the police system and to restructure it on attainment of independence should be recorded as one of the serious mistakes responsible for the inadequacies in meeting the problems of violence. Even with the police system devised more than a century ago, it should have been possible to do better if only the police forces in the states had retained their discipline, commitment to their professional obligations, integrity of the leadership and line of command. Unfortunately, there has been severe erosion of each of these values arising from the debilitating nexus between the police and the politicians. This dealt a further below to the outmoded police system crying for reform.

This has been further compounded by the judicial system which was originally conceived and established, like the police, to suit socio-economic conditions and political ethos different from the post-independence era. While the separation of the judiciary from the executive made the judiciary independent, which is a very desirable judicial concept, adequate provision was not made simultaneously to ensure dispensation of speedy justice to tens of thousands of supplicants who converge on the courts in the hope of receiving quick and fair disposal of their complaints. The increased pressure of litigation was a direct outcome of the socio-economic changes that swept the countryside.

The techniques devised for meeting the problems of a country at a point of time in its history which had been found, successful may not work under changed conditions. The Roman empire had evolved an almost perfect legal, military, and economic techniques for maintaining law and order, defending itself against external enemies, and managing the production and exchange of goods. But in the third century, these very institutions which were considered near-perfect proved inadequate to prevent civil wars, invasion by the Barbarians and depreciation of the currency because new events had rendered the existing institutions ineffective.

The deficiencies or the inadequacy or even the inappropriateness of the institutions which are expected to look after the problems caused by the socio-economic changes in the country have unfortunately given rise to distorted perception of the realities on the ground to the political executive. This is turn has set in motion a series of administrative and executive actions which are not compatible with democratic processes. This is noticeable in the political reactions to the demands of the weaker sections, which militate against vested interests. Proper enforcement of the Minimum Wages Act or the tenurial rights is an important obligation which the weaker sections expect the Government agencies to fulfil. If, however, this is not done either due to indifference of the enforcing agencies or their collusion with vested interests, there is a very real danger of disenchantment of the affected population with the Government who may even suspect the motives of the Government. By the use of force in such a situation by the Government agencies against the weaker sections, accusing them of being Naxalites or belonging to other ideologically motivated groups, the Government exposes itself to the charge of colluding with vested interests and going against the weaker sections. This is the dilemma that right-thinking individuals face when they survey the rural scenes involving violence in the States of Uttar Pradesh, Bihar and Andhra Pradesh among others.

The deficiencies of the institutional arrangement with regad to the implementation of the several well-conceived programmes to improve the economic condition of the weaker sections will be evident from the following which is extracted from an evaluation study of the Employment Guarantee Scheme in Maharashtra, quoted by D. Bandopadhyay, Secretary Rural Development Ministry, Government of India, in the Convention Papers compiled following the National Convention of Indian Society for Training and Development in December 1984-January 1985. "The Maharashtra Employment Guarantee Scheme evaluation study brought out certain distortions in the implementation of the programme. Share of the non-target group in employment was significantly higher than that of the target group (agricultural workers and marginal farmers). The study concluded 'EGS had catered more to the cultivators of higher holding groups than the requiremnts of landless agricultural labour or smaller cultivator household'. Sharing of benefits of the assets created through EGS was more skewed than the sharing of employment. According to the joint evaluation, as many as 91% of user household belonged to the category of cultivators. The next important category being agricultural labourers formed about 6%. It was further observed that the benefits of EGS assets had gone to a large extent to the medium and large farmers. The small and marginal farmers constitute only 21% of user households"......

Commenting generally, D. Bandopadhyay has observed, "Because of lack of knowledge and confidence on the part of the beneficiaries and because of absence of institutional support, a whole host of development of middle men have sprung up who cheat the beneficiaries in the name of illegal gains with the bureaucracy to facilitate sanction or aceptance of household oriented schemes. The situation calls for urgent remedy."

Defeudalising a traditional set up is not a process which can be completed instantly. Even if external and tangible manifestations of feudalism are dismantled, it is not equally easy to remove the mental cobwebs, reform and refine the mental attitude of the people who have stood to lose in the new dispensation. Even if they part with all that has been legislated out of them, they are not likely to adjust themselves to the new relationship between persons and between different groups which the socio-economic changes have brought about. The hangover of feudalism will take a long time to disappear. In the meantime it lingers on with effects which can take diverse forms and patterns distorting human relationships and giving rise to violence.

"No society is strong which does not acknowledge the protesting man. And no man is human who does not draw strength from the natural animal".[1] In this context, it would be worthwhile to bear in mind the history of our country during the British period. We as a people have in a sense already gone through a situation during the pre-Inde-pendenc days, comparable to the one that the weaker sections are presently going through. For instance there was the Rowlatt Act which had a brief but ignoble life span. From the point of view of the framers of that Act, any form of protest against misrule and high-handedness was seen to be conspiratorial and seditious. In a different context, we would do well to guard ourselves against labelling of even normal and legitimate reactions against some of the prevailing injustice as conspiracies hatched or acts inspired by Naxalities. Once the Indian Police, as it is presently constituted, realises what the Government expects and wants in terms of law and order, it will stop short of nothing to please the Government. In contingencies of this type when heads have to roll to achieve results, heads do start rolling with increasing velocity. In this context the observations of Pandit Motilal Nehru on the Rowlatt Act, made during his presidential address at the Amritsar Congress in 1919 would be of relevance : "No one can but deplore violence and political crime. But let us not forget that this is the outcome of continued repression. It is due to the perversity of the Executive which blinds itself to the cause of the discontent and like a mad bull goes about attacking all who dare stand up against it."

In a democratic society it is essential to ensure that the reaction of the state to violence indulged in by ideologically motivated groups does not degenerate into a form of counter-terror. The state through its instruments such as the police, should not itself practice the very cult of violence that it accuses offenders of practising.

In the rural scene in India, vast changes have come about during the last three decades. No single measure has released such complex and far reaching forces as the introduction of adult franchise for elections to Panchayats, local bodies, State Legislatures and the Parliament. The new administrative functionaries like the Gram Sevak, the Village Acount or the Lekha Pal and others in the rural hierarchy who have been introduced to administer welfare and administrative units, educational institutions, primary health centures, rural development organisations and the anti-poverty programmes have created an impact on the socio-economic set up of the villages. The improvement in agricultural inputs and extension services have produced their own effect on agricultural and allied activities. The halting and evasive manner in which the land reforms were implemented have created certain tensions. The creation of several infrastructures such as irrigation, facilities for setting up cottage industries have brought about a visible change in the countryside. The poor sections of the cultivating tenants who did not have enough cash for acquiring ownership of the land, had either to borrow money or had to deny themselves tenurial security and had to become non-owning backdoor tenants. This had created its own hazards, harassments and uncertainties. All the changes while creating several centres of power also created focii of tension between the several competing and conflicting groups.

There is promise of ushering in an equitable society and for which efforts have also been initiated. What is more, the people who stand to benefit by these are becoming aware of the utter iniquity of the system that they had lived through. They have come to believe the promises of the State as enshrined in our Constitution, to eradicate these iniquities and the distortions in the socio-economic life of the millions that had been an integral part of the system inherited by Independent India. In the context of the promises and the programmes in the post-Independence period, the very same iniquities, indignities and injustices seem unendurable now to the same millions who till not very long ago had accepted and resigned themselves to the pernicious socio-economic system as something ordained by God and hence inevitable. Equality of political rights and socio-economic exploitation cannot go together. The same millions have now become aware of the fact that they do not necessarily have to traverse through the travails which their forefathers had gone through over the centuries. The evils that have been removed from the system to the extent possible during the post-Indpendence decades have only heightened the consciousness among the affected of the evils that continue to persist. It is true that the evils have diminished but the sensitivity has become more acute and to that extent the clamour for relief more strident and at times even violent.

References

1. J. Bronowski : "The Face of Violence : An Essay with Play."

PART III

CHAPTER 5

GAP BETWEEN PROMISE AND PERFORMANCE - LAND REFORMS, GENERAL :

That a study on the subject of violence in India should contain a reference at some length to the status of Land Reforms needs some explanation. Land Reforms is one area in which there has been considerable double talk at responsible levels, if not double think. The spirit in which the Land Reforms were conceived and legislation was enacted was not the spirit in which the state governments got down to the job of implementation. Here was one area in some of the states where political power was in tacit collusion with economic power in utter disregard of what was announced from the political platforms by political leaders in pursuance of the national policy, when it came to giving effect to these declared policies and statutes, the vested interests wielding political power thwarted proper implementation of the reforms, through subterfuges to which bureaucrats were also a party. Even so, the imperatives of the agrarian reforms, even to the extent to which they have been implemented, have brought about a change in society, though not a transformation of the social order. An effort will be made to examine some of the gaps between the promises and their fulfilment which has contributed to social tensions and violence in the rural areas.

Agrarian Reform is a comprehensive concept and is composed of several elements. Some of these are: redistribution of land among the landless, security of tenure, creation of individual ownership, security of rentals, favourable and easily available credit facilities, easy availability of the several agricultural inputs required for modern methods of farming and cooperative marketing facilities. While each of these components is important in its own way, ownership of the land, and in its absence, the security of tenure are the two elements which set the pace of the rest of the reforms. Though these aspects had been taken care of in the land reforms legislation in different states, there is still considerable weakness, ambiguity and even deliberate negligence in practice in some of the states, particularly Bihar and Uttar Pradesh. As long as the security of tenure and certainty of rent are not assured unambiguously, the potential for violence in the rural areas of the country will continue to exist. By keeping alive the uncertainties with regard to the tenure and the rent, the State opens itself to the charge of encouraging a society based on iniquity and exploitation in stead of fostering the formation of a society based on social justice and equity. A categorical assertion in these matters is possible only through the political will of the Government. This in turn depends on the source from which it derives its political strength and sustenance. As it happened in the decades immediately following the declaration of Independence, the ruling party had derived its legislative and political support from the very segments of society which had had a vested interest in retaining the economic power arising out of the ownership of large land holdings. Land reforms legislation and its implementation which affect this landed class which constitutes one of the most important centres of power have therefore been successfully thwarted by it. The Government of Bihar, and to an extent Uttar Pradesh, have not taken the objective of the land legislation to its logical conclusion as this would have inevitably alienated the major source from which the Governments have been deriving political support.

Mrs. Gandhi addressing the Chief Ministers' Conference in November, 1969 observed : "The warning of the time is that unless the Green Revolution is accompanied by a revolution based on social justice, I am afraid the Green Revolution may not remain green." Mrs. Indira Gandhi wanted Chief Ministers to "act now, when there is still time and hope..... No single programme so intimately affects so many millions of our people as land reforms." In an allusion to the land grabs that was taking place in several states during 1969, Mrs. Indira Gandhi observed: "political parties may organize, even exploit rural discontent but they do not create it. The time has come to face the facts.... the land reform measures implemented have failed to match the legitimate expectations which were first forstered among million of cultivators during the national movement.... In short, we have yet to create institutional conditions which would enable small farmers, tenants and landless labourers to share in the agricultural new deal."[1]

The status of land reforms as it existed on the eve of the Sixth Five Year Plan in 1980 was described as follows: "Often the necessary determination has been lacking to effectively undertake action particularly in the matter of implementation of ceiling laws, consolidation of holdings and in not vigorously pursuing the concealed tenancies and having them vested with tenancy/occupacy rights as enjoined under the Act."[2] This was again referred to on the occasion of the Conference of the Revenue Ministers held in New Delhi on 18th May, 1985. The minutes of this Conference clearly show that there are even now informal, unsecured tenants and even tenants holding their land on oral agreements and share-croppers who are not on record.

In the course of his speech at the Conference of Revenue Ministers in 1985, the Union Agriculture Minister observed: "Considerable gaps exist between the area estimated as surplus and area actually declared as surplus, the area declared surplus and the area taken possession of; the area taken possession of and the area actually distributed........ Adequate protection has to be provided to the beneficiary by the Government. The *Entente Cordiale* that exists between the local revenue staff and the rural rich is a major inhibiting factor. Nearly 6.55 lakh hectares of land is locked in litigation in spite of the constitutional protection given to the various Ceiling Laws."[3]

Here is proof, if proof was ever needed, of the collusion in the rural areas between the Government functionaries andthe vested interests, a fact which has been acknowledged at the Central level at a very responsible and formal forum.

Occasionally there is an unholy alliance between responsible Government functionaries and vested interests at the cutting edge. When it goes further and leads to wrecking vengence against those who are protesting against the denial of their legitimate dues, the deprived sections sometimes get dubbed as Naxalites.

According to the Agricultural Census of 1980-1981, holdings below 2 hectares form 74.5% of the total number of operational holdings but account for 26.3% of the area only. Holdings above 10 hectares, though constituting only 2.4% of the total number of holdings, cover 22.8% area. Thus, concentration of land in big land holdings is still very much in evidence. In effect it has created in the countryside, pockets of land owners with strong economic base which in turn has promoted their social and political influence.

After 1972 National Guidelines, the State Governments estimated that about 23.54 lakh hectares would be surplus. The position in 1985 January was : the area declared surplus was only 17.46 lakh hectares. Area taken possession of was 12.11 lakh hectares and the area distributed was 9.02 lakh hectares. The area taken possession of is 72.6% of the area declared surplus and the area distributed is 51.7% of the area declared surplus and 74.3% of the area taken possession of. Scheduled Castes and Scheduled Tribe beneficiaries together represent 54.1% of the allottes and account for 50.5% of the area alloted.[4] Statewise figures may be seen at Annexure C1 and C2. This refers to the position as it stood in 1983.

The agrarian reforms in their multi-dimensional aspects brought the Scheduled Castes and the Scheduled Tribes too into the economic mainstream. This is indicated by the percentage of Scheduled Castes and Scheduled Tribes dependent on agriculture as revealed by the Census of 1961, 1971 and 1981 (Annexures A, B and C). Though the number of Scheduled Castes and Scheduled Tribes dependent on agricultural activities declined marginally in 1981 when compared with 1971 Census, the fact remains that their dependence on agriculture continues to be heavy.

The Annexure at C1 and C2 give the percentage of Scheduled Castes and Scheduled Tribes to the total agricultural labour in the different states along with the percentage of land allotted to them. Since the bulk of these Scheduled Castes and Scheduled Tribes are dependent on agricultural labour, it is imperative that the prescribed minimum wages rules are enforced strictly through appropriately designed administrative machinery. Any effort at depriving them of their legitimate wages will only fuel further tensions between them and those for whom they work. The discontent generated provide content and justification for the ideologies of certain political parties to exploit the conditions to pursue their plans of action. This is already in evidence in parts of Bihar and Uttar Pradesh.

The problems stemming from agrarian reforms are in a sense the first-time problems of Independent India. The failure of the Government to provide a proper forum which could or should have resolved the difficulties arising from the implementation of the land reforms promptly has resulted in heavy litigation involving tens of thousands of cases which have dragged on for years with the end nowhere in sight. In the process, the poor among the contenders who had longingly hoped for a better, happier and more settled tomorrow have only got themselves entangled in harassing and interminable court cases.

Law and order receive priority over the enforcement of land reform laws as far as the state governments are concerned. In states where they are politically strong, the vested interests ensure that enforcement of the laws is impeded or evaded in one way or another. Wherever ideological support is provided to the affected poor classes by the intervention of political parties committed to the welfare of the rural poor, they usually get on the wrong side of the Government either by their own zeal for the cause, which often out-runs their discretion, or by landing themselves in situations which have been cleverly contrived for them by the vested interests. The absence of an organized and strong pressure group on behalf of the landless and the weaker sections has in fact resulted in failure to press the implementation of the relevant laws to the logical conclusion. Gunnar Myrdal has rightly observed in his book: 'Asian Drama': "Fundamental reforms that will break stagnation in rural India must be sustained by pressure from below."

The Commission for Scheduled Castes and Scheduled Tribes in its 5th report (March, 1983)[5] had concluded that in many States the necessary political will to implement the land reforms was singularly lacking. Even in cases where land was alloted to the Scheduled Scheduled Castes and Scheduled Tribes, the beneficiaries were not in actual possession and enjoyment of the same as the erstwhile owners had adopted unfair methods including recourse to judicial process to deprive the deemed beneficiaries the benefits of land ownership. Even inclusion of various land reform laws in the 9th Schedule of the Constitution had not helped in carrying forward measures and judicial processes are still being widely used by the land owning classes to defeat these measures.

The Commission has gone on to observe that the land declared surplus and taken possession of by the State Government are understandably marginal lands with extremely poor productivity. Some outlay for the development of the lands and certain inputs in the shape of fertilizers, seeds, pesticides etc. will be needed to make their cultivation viable. Though there is a scheme for central financial assistance in this regard, no proper use is being made of this facility. In certain states, the allotment of land is the responsibility of the Revenue Department whereas the provision of inputs falls within the jurisdiction of the Agricultural Department and there was no coordination between the two.

The Raj Krishna Committee on Land Reforms[6] appointed in 1978 had observed in one of its reports : "In spite of the existence of article 31-A, 31-B and 9th Schedule, the fact remains that a large number of writ petitions pertaining to land reform laws and their application are awaiting disposal in High Courts. Some of them have been pending for longer periods. The result is that land owners continue to be in possession of land held to be transferable to the landless. Tenants have also been denied for long periods rights to which they were entitled under tenancy laws. In spite of the economic weakness of tenants, they have been involved in prolonged and prohibitively costly litigations. Therefore, it has become necessary to take some measures urgently to speed up the final disposal of all pending land reform cases at all levels. Otherwise, the promise of improving the status of tenants and the redistribution of lands among the landless may continue to remain unfulfilled." If for this purpose a constitutional amendment is necessary, it should be undertaken. Denying a person or group of individuals their legitimate entitlements is a kind of disguised violence which can have as pernicious an effect as manifest violence.

The very practical and salutary recommendations of the Raj Krishna Committee do not appear to have made any difference to the mode and manner of handling the problems relating to land reforms. No special efforts have been made by the State Governments pursuant to the Committee's report.

The steps which if implemented properly and correctly, are capable of reducing rural tensions are :

1) Certainty regarding tenurial rights to prevent arbitrary dispossessions;

2) Reasonable rent levels;
3) Conferment of homestead rights to the landless;
4) Enforcement of the Ceiling Laws and distribution of the available surplus among the landless.

To quote the Minutes of the Revenue Ministers' Conference of 1985: "Sizeable areas in Andhra Pradesh, Haryana, Punjab, Bihar, Uttar Pradesh and West Bengal have gone out of the total quantum of surplus land as a result of court decisions. Even land already distributed had to be denotified in many cases causing considerable hardship to the assignees who had invested their resources."[7] Such a state of affairs need not have come about if the land reforms had been accompanied by a strong institutional back up.

There seems to be a distinct lack of the requisite political will and administrative commitment and impartiality required to implement the reforms. Heightened political consciousness and the success of agitational methods in securing reforms elsewhere will continue to strengthen political movements on agrarian issues.

Due to inadequacy, ineffectiveness or even partisanship of the enforcement machinery, agricultural labour which remains unorganised in most of the states continues to receive wages below the prescribed minimum. Due to non-availability of regular employment during most part of the year, the agricultural workers have no choice but to accept wages lower than minimum. The Commission for Scheduled Castes and Scheduled Tribes has observed: "It is most unfortunate that even prescription of minimum wages, leave aside their actual payment, has been the cause of infliction of the most inhuman atrocities on the helpless agricultural labour when they dare to demand the minimum wage prescribed by Government officials."[8] These ameliorative measures which are intrinsically good fail in their implementation for want of sincerity of purpose. That they are more often projected with a view to derive political mileage rather than achieving social objectives is evident from the observations made by the Commission for Scheduled Castes and Scheduled Tribes in its 5th report with regard to the small size of the house-sites allotted to Scheduled Castes and Scheduled Tribes. The Commission has observed: "The living area in several cases was not more than 10 feet by 10 feet. How a family consisting of husband, wife and two or three children is expected to live in this small place is beyond our comprehension. When we pleaded with a Chief Minister that the living area provided to a family should consist of at least two rooms, he pleaded paucity of financial resources. When we suggested reduction in the number of houses, he thought that we were being blind to his political compulsions. According to him, it is essentially a game of numbers and no Chief Minister would be prepared to reduce the number of houses and make them larger and of better specifications, since he would be unable to satisfy the large number of beneficiaries and this would be politically suicidal to him. The fact that in this process, public money is being wasted merely to reach an unrealistic target did not seem to concern him very much."[9]

H. Pais who is the Dean of the National Labour Institute, Delhi in his paper prepared in December, 1986 on "Unorganised Labour" has observed: "Minimum wages fixed by the centre and state governments fall far below the poverty line.... Labour administration particularly that relating to the unorganised sector has remained more or less static in comparison with the size of the problem and its growing needs.... Our paper has clearly brought out the linkages between an equitable wage policy for the unorganised sector and development. In fact, in the absence of an equitable wage policy, integrated with other developmental inputs, the expectations in the Seventh Five Year Plan regarding crossing of the poverty line by a major chunk of the population in the unorganised sector might prove to be a myth...... Conditions of agricultural labour cannot improve unless they are organised. The manner of their organisation should be the primary concern of the state but generally governments have failed to discharge their responsibilities in this area mainly because of the social structure which dominates and controls the government apparatus."

Since the transfer of more than a very small part of landless labour to non-agricultural sectors will not be easy or even feasible in the immediate future, the demand for adequate wages and fuller employment in the agricultural sector has become a very vital issue. The fact which has to be faced squarely is that if the security of tenure for a relatively small number of tenants has not made any impact even after all these years, State action to enforce minimum wages for agricultural labour is likely to face much greater resistance than is being faced now.

On land reforms and its implementation, it is worth quoting the observations of Shri P.S. Appu, the ex-Chief Secretary of Bihar, who having held important posts under the Central Government had chosen premature retirement from the I.A.S, and who is an acknowledged authority on land reforms : "In no sphere of public activity in our country since Independence has the hiatus between precepts and practice, between policy pronouncements and actual execution been as great as in the domain of land reforms. With resolute and unambiguous political will, all the other short-comings and difficulties could have been overcome; in the absence of such will even minor obstacles have become formidable road-blocks in the path of Indian land reforms. Considering the characteristic of the political power structure obtaining in the country, it was only natural that the required political will was not forth-coming."

References

1. The Selected papers of Wolf Ladejinsky: Agrarian Reforms - an unfinished business - Edited by Louis Walinsky (1977).
2. Minutes of the Conference of the Revenue Ministers held in New Delhi on 18th May, 1985.
3. IBID.
4. IBID.
5. Report of the Commission for Scheduled Castes and Scheduled Tribes–April 1982– March 1983 - Vth report.

6. The Raj Krishna Committee Report on Land Reforms (1978).
7. Minutes of the Conference of the Revenue Ministers held in New Delhi on 18th May, 1985.
8. Report of the Commission for Scheduled Castes and Scheduled Tribes- April 1982 - March 1983 - Vth Report.
9. IBID.

CHAPTER 6

LAND REFORMS IN BIHAR

Feudalism with all that it signifies in human relations, which continues to be a lingering aspect of the socio-economic life of Bihar, can be better understood in the context of the conditions that prevailed in Bihar prior to the introduction of the land reforms. This will be evident from the following which is based on the paper authored by Francine R. Frankel, 1984.[1]

"Under the permanent settlement full priprietory rights in over 90% of the cultivated land were conferred on a small class of Zamindars - perhaps 4% of the population...... The new class of Zamindars and their agents were armed with formidable powers...... While it proved easy to use British authority to intimidate the ryot, the same power appeared impotent to protect him. The Zamindars frequently ignored the Government regulations to give the tenants written pattas stipulating the rent and other conditions of the lease..... Political advantages to the State of the growing Government-Zamindar alliance were purchased at a very high cost to the majority of the peasantry. By the 1870s the "high-handed abuses" of the Zamindars had reduced the cultivators of Bihar to a "state of extreme depression and misery" which marked them as "the most wretched class" we find in this country.... Agricultural labourers whose wages were paid in kind lived in some areas in a kind of social thraldom, some times selling themselves, their wives and children to life long servitude for paltry sums."

The Brahmins, the Bumihars, the Rajputs and the Kayasthas, who constitute what has come to be referred to as the upper castes have traditionally owned the major share of the land in the State of Bihar. Members of these communities had held traditionally senior and responsible positions in the administration, in professions and in politics. In the new socio-economic dispensation in the wake of independence, a small segment of the Scheduled Castes and Scheduled Tribes who have been able to get a share in the administrative positions and who with that strength have moved up the socio-economic ladder, have so far failed to dislodge the upper castes from the strategic positions that they hold in the politics and administration of the State. It will take quite some time before they are able to do so assuming that in the meantime nothing happens which may give a set back to the upward mobility of the backward communities.

The Yadavs, Koeris and Kurmis by virtue of the land that they acquired as cultivators at the time of the abolition of the Zamindari system have become a new class of haves pitted against the have-nots. The Zamindars used to get their land cultivated by the members of these comunities who over a period of time had become efficient agriculturists. These cultivators became owners of the land as a result of the land reforms and were the classes who stood to gain more than anyone else. Thus, these caste groups improved their relative economic and social position; and their large numbers give them positive strength under the adult suffrage.

Thousands of unaccounted tenants were deprived of their holdings during the long time gap between the enactment of land reform legislations and its implementation. As late as in 1970, it was possible to find ex-intermediaries in possession of estates extending over 5,000 acres or more resorting to various devices to hold on to the land. The manner in which the enactment of the land ceiling Act was delayed, and the number of loop-holes it carried with it when eventually passed, are a measure of the power and influence that the large land holders wielded at the administrative and political levels in Bihar. The upper limit of the ceiling was more with reference to the individual than the family as a unit. Benami transfers proliferated. Every conceivable ploy was devised by the owners to escape from the provisions of the Land Ceiling Act. Provisions were made for orchards, pastures and even for animals which were treated as pets! The law allowed each land owner a period of six months to enable him to transfer the land to those entitled to it through inheritance. Notice of enforcement of the 1962 Act was issued as late as in 1965 giving adequate time to the landlords to evade the provisions. There was also a provision for the tenant to surrender the land voluntarily which could then be settled with another tenant. This provision has been the cause of a large number of disputes giving rise to considerable violence in the rural areas.[2]

In Bihar, the estimated surplus land under the Ceiling Act should have been, as per the Agricultural Census 1976-1977, about 11.29 lakh acres. But the estimate given by the State Government on 1-1-1984 was only 2.99 lakh acres. Out of the declared surplus of 2.99 lakh acres, 1.9 lakh acres were distributed. Total land involved in litigation was 77,500 acres.

"In Begusarai district, 2,108 acres of land were allotted to Harijans out of 9,000 acres of land declared surplus following enforcement of ceilings. 26,129 possession slips were issued to landless persons including 9,490 Harijans. But till May, 1979 only 950 persons were able to secure physical possession of the land allotted to them. The reason for this delay was stated to be the fact that the revenue records were not up to date as land survey had not been undertaken for many years in most of the districts."[3]

The only visible consequence of Zamindari abolition can be said to be the reduction in the number of large holdings. But even this could well be a matter of credit for the manner in which the provisions of the Act were successfully defeated by the Zamindars by distribution among the several members of the families, according to the maximum admissible limits.

A Government working group evaluating the implementation of the land reforms in 1973 had observed: "By their abysmal failure to implement the laws, the authorities in Bihar have reduced the whole package of land reform measures to a sour joke. This emboldened the land owning class to treat the entire agrarian reforms with utter contempt. Elsewhere in the country, the law evaders have a sneaking respect for the law enforcing authorities. Their approach is furtive, their method clandestine. In Bihar, the land owners do not care a tuppence for the administration. Their modus operandi open and insolent."[4]

According to the Agricultural Census of Bihar done in 1980-1981, 75.5% of the holdings (83,20,600) of less than one hectare each are marginal holdings covering 26.7% of the area. As against this 6% (68,100) large holdings covering more than ten hectares account for 10.5% of the total operational area of the State. Out of the total operational holdings of 1,10,29,600 the Scheduled Castes' share comes to 9,28,061 which works out to 8.41% of the holdings. The operational area covered by the holdings of the Scheduled Castes works out to 4.56% of the total operated area in the State. The figures for the Scheduled Tribes is 8,28,399 holdings which is 7.21% of the total holdings in the State covering an operational area of 16.24%. Though seemingly well off, the figures indicating the Scheduled Tribes' share apparently do not take into account the fact that a good part of the land legally owned by the Scheduled Tribes had actually got alienated to non-Tribals. However, as a subterfuge and a legal fiction this fact is not reflected in the Government records as the alienation of land is not permissible under the law and hence not recordable. The Commission for Scheduled Castes and Scheduled Tribes has stated in its 5th report that in Bihar 52,127 cases of tribal land which was alienated involving an area of 76,411 acres had been registered and in 27,454 cases the decision was in favour of restoration of land to the Tribals. The area in question was 32,636 acres. Getting such a decision from the Government is one side of the coin, but the actual restoration of the land and its enjoyment is another. As a matter of fact, only in 1,774 cases had land been actually and physically restored to the tribals out of 27,454. Even out of the total holdings of the Scheduled Castes, 89.3% fall in the category of marginal holdings below one hectare, covering an area of 51.8% of the total area and 6.3% fall within the category of one to two hectares, covering an area of 15.6% of the total area belonging to the Scheduled Castes. The figures for the Scheduled Tribes under the same head comes to 51.3% covering an area of 10.3% of the total area and 15.9% covering an area of 10.4% of the total area.

The system of share-cropping which is prevalent in parts of Bihar has several sinister aspects. The land owners do not allow the share-croppers to cultivate the same land in successive years. This is because of the fear among the land owners that if the share-croppers are allowed to cultivate the same land in consecutive years, they may stake their claim for occupancy rights. Though according to law, the land owner is entitled to only ¼th of the produce, in actual fact the land owners insist and take half the produce. With no security of tenure and no bargaining power, the share-croppers are entirely at the mercy of the land owners. Most of the share-croppers belong to the Scheduled Castes and the Scheduled Tribes or other backward castes. In some of the districts of Bihar, the share-cropping system has given rise to considerable rural tensions culminating in bloodshed.

Anand Chakravarti[5] writing in the Economic and Political Weekly dated October 25, 1986 has observed that the belligerence of the land owners in general in contemporary Bihar is so very blatant that even the working committee group on land reforms of the National Commission on Agriculture had observed on the basis of experience in some areas of Bihar that "land owners are organised and aggressive........ with an obliging administration on their side, they are definitely not going to give up an iota of their rights, privileges and economic dominance without a stiff fight..... no law, however, good it may be in conferring on paper, rights, title and interest on the bataidars, will have the slightest chance of success unless the bataidars have a strong and militant mass organisation of their own, capable of not only defending their own rights given by the law – but also capable of mounting counter-action to prevent and forestall any direct attack on them."

Ladejinsky observes: "What is crucial is that in Bihar the leading politicians have not really accepted the idea of change as a means to improve the conditions of the tenure. And yet, only they are the authentic makers or unmakers of reforms."

According to the agenda papers for the Conference of the Revenue Secretaries and Revenue Ministers dated 24th and 25th November, 1986, a Bill to amend the Bihar Tenancy Act to confer ownership rights on share croppers has been drafted[6]. It remains to be seen to what extent this Bill when enacted will be allowed to be implemented by the vested interests who wield political clout arising from affluence based on land assets.

According to the report brought out by the Revenue and Land Reforms Department of the Government of Bihar for the year 1983-1984, the position with regard to the disposal of cases involving the share-croppers is, total cases which related to the share croppers on March 9, 1984 were 58,860 of which 16,622 cases were decided in favour of Bataidars (share-croppers), 33,283 were decided against Bataidars and the cases pending were 8,955.

As far as the Scheduled Tribes are concerned, land belonging to them had been encroached upon by non-tribals. The position with regard to the extent of the area pending settlement was 14,038.38 acres involving 10,617 cases in 1983-1984. Out of these cases that had been decided upto 1983-1984 were 4,434 involving an area of 5,417 acres of which 2,497 cases were decided in favour of the Tribals involving an area of 2296 acres and 1,937 cases involving

3,121 acres went against the Tribals. The remaining cases were pending. Considering the very large number of cases that have gone against the weaker sections, one wonders whether the institutional arrangement provided for the settling of such cases which can make all the difference between destitution and subsistence are really in tune with the spirit of the land legislations.

In the absence of periodical land surveys, it is very difficult to fix the land ownership and more so in the crime-ridden vast 'Diara' area of the State. The boundaries even if fixed are washed away by flood and by sowing time the next season, there is practically no sign whatsoever left to prove ownership. In such a situation might is right and violence is inherent. What has changed the situation sharply in the recent years is the induction of muscle men by the different parties to the dispute.

The dispute over land which is primarily of a civil nature is very often converted into a criminal case by some overt criminal act on the part of one of the parties. The calculated move to bring a criminal element into the transaction is to give the case a criminal dimension in the hope that it would get a comparatively speedy disposal. I was told by a top police official in Patna that thousands of cases of land disputes are pending over several years with no hope of the issues being resolved in the foreseable future. Hence their recourse to action coming within the criminal law in the hope that at least the original land dispute which may have been hanging fire over the years may get resolved one way or the other. The result has been a colossal increase in the number of criminal cases and mounting pressure on the already over worked criminal courts.

At the same time Bihar provides a very revealing example of how and when the political will and administrative commitment converge with a sense purpose, even seemingly difficult issues that have defied solution over several years and have generated needless and mindless violence, become resolvable issues within the capability of the functionaries in the administration. The three issues of debt redemption, occupancy rights of share croppers and higher wages for agricultural labourers have generally sharpened the antagonism between the peasants and the land owners, and generated considerable violence. During the national Emergency of 1975-1976 when every aspect of administration was totally set on producing certain desirable and demonstrable results, 50,000 acres of surplus land were acquired in Bihar in marked contrast to the acquisition of a mere 9,700 acres under the Ceiling Laws over all the years prior to the Emergency. The State Government also received 20,431 acres under the voluntary surrender scheme which called upon the big landlords to see the writing on the wall and disclose their surplus holdings. About 10,000 acres of acquired land were redistributed.

Agricultural wages were first fixed under the Minimum Wages Act in 1948 and revised in 1966-1967. They were however not implemented even in a single village in Bihar. They were again revised in 1974-75. In the 19 months of the Emergency, 68,000 agricultural labourers were helped to get arrears of wages totalling Rupees 1 crore from the land owners. Indebtedness of agricultural labourers and poor peasants totalling Rupees 4.5 crores were written off and redemption certificates were issued. The achievements during the Emergency amply demonstrated that we as a nation are capable of doing even the right things only under duress and under fear of being called upon to account for failure to fulfil targets. It is a sad commentary on the working of the political-administrative system that a draconic Emergency regime should be necessary to produce results which ought to be attainable through normal processes and functioning. When will we do the right things only because they have to be done, and not because we have to render an account of our having done them?

There are three types of land relationships in Bihar, each of which has been the cause of considerable violence in the rural areas. The intermediate class of land owners most of whom belonging to the backward communities, enjoy certainty of tenancy or ownership. They cultivate the land, work hard and have emerged as a force in the rural as also the urban life of Bihar. Their land holdings are by and large within ceiling limits. This class consists largely of Kurmis and Yadavs. This is one stablising factor in rural Bihar though this also has a de-stabilising aspect to the extent it has led to increasing conflict with the landless who work in their lands. A good part of Naxalite activities are centered in the districts of Bhojpur, Rohtas, Aurangabad and Gaya. Certain pockets in the districts of Patna and Nalanda are also affected.

The second category of land relationship refers to the first generation land owners who have come by their small or marginal holdings by way of gift from Bhoodan movement or as a result of re-distribution of a part of the land declared surplus when the Ceiling Act was given effect to, even though partially and with reservations. Mostly the Harijans fall in this category, some of whom may have come by their possessions after considerable court proceedings. They expect to hold on to their land against all efforts to dispossess them. In the process, they find themselves more vulnerable than they would have been if they had been without their little possessions of land.

The bigger land owners constitute the third source of land relationship. They have the bulk of the land carried over from the days of the abolition of the Zamindari system and have retained their hold over their land in spite of the Ceiling Act. When they deny the minimum wages to the landless peasants, we hear of the peasants organising themselves under the leadership of the Naxalites or picking up an open fight with the land owners and making examples of the selected among them by attacking their farms and killing them. The land owners as also the peasants who are pitted against them hold fire arms illegally and they conspire against each other for revenge which leads to a chain of violence. It is the conflict between these two groups which is the source of much violence.

If the State of Bihar is to be rid of the types and quantum of violence which today characterises the horizon, it will require the political and administrative will, coming together in all honesty in an effort to deal squarely with the problem.

The Bihar land holder is also sometimes the contractor in which capacity he has access to public funds. The extra profit that he makes over and above the legitimate share is used to make illegal payments for either terrorising or bribing the officials. The land holders are also a vote-bank which function they fulfil through their hold on the Mukhias (leaders) of the villages. The Mukhias make sure that the weaker sections of people who are dependent or beholden to them in several ways are the captive voters of the party or of the candidates supported by the land owners.

Most political parties which happen to be in power at any time do not have their organizational reach in the State to the grass-root level in the villages in a structured and disciplined hierarchical form. This gap which is very serious even in normal times assumes additional significance in the days immediately preceding the elections as also during periods of uncertain political situations which, as it happens in Bihar is a chronic and continuous problem. The void is generally sought to be filled by the political leadership by utilising intermediate groups of landowners and other influential segments such as businessmen and contractors. These agents, if they are to be useful at the time of elections, and at other critical times, have to be kept happy and contented at all times. There is a price to be paid for such support which requires the Government to turn a blind eye towards their questionable dealings which may sometimes even be blatantly illegal. This takes many forms. There are mafia leaders who have to be kept contented by letting them carry on their nefarious activities through which they generate money power. Contracts are given to mafia leaders against all norms of propriety. In one case reported from Dhanbad district, when it was pointed out that the person to whom a particular contract, involving a very large sum of money, was being paid was not a desirable character, the chief political functionary of the time is reported to have said : "I have to purchase my political power." Having purchased it by such dubious means, such political power can only be used for dubious ends.

The iniquities that are associated with the rural life of Bihar are the end results of vested interests operating from positions of strength and free from the restraining influence of law and authority. Since they have taken care of the needs of political operators at State level they conduct themselves as though they are not answerable to anybody. The caste ridden society of Bihar ensures that the Government functionaries in different departments extend the requisite help to the politicians belonging to the respective castes, unmindful of their own departmental and disciplinary constraints. Postings of Government officials are often governed by caste considerations.

In an arrangement where centres of power proliferate and each such centre constitutes a pressure group, they have no qualms about using the police or the administrative machinery for subserving sectional, sectarian, caste or group interests. This, ironically enough, has led to an accretion in the influence of the police which does not legitimately belong to it, but which it has acquired over a period by operating outside its legally recognised limits. This has ushered in a culture of mutual support and dependence between the policc and the pressure groups. This nexus between the police, the politicians and their cohorts is a glaring fact in Bihar. An arrangement that thrives by acquiring power through questionable means and then using it through coteries and vested interests inevitably leads to wrong and distorted perception of human activities and events. This in turn does not help the powers at responsible levels to understand correctly the signals that emanate from the villages. This results very often in the State machinery shooting down the messenger in the belief that in the process the message itself has been killed. Many of the problems of Bihar can be attributed to this sad misunderstanding.

Another effect of such a venal administrative set up is that a large chunk of population who are socially and economically backward are not the real beneficiaries of the Government's programmes such as minimum wages, health and education. Until only a few years back they had resigned themselves to this fate. However, during the last decade or so the worm has begun to turn. The youth among the Harijans have woken up to their rights and are prepared to fight for them. They are no longer reconciled to their old fatalistic style of living. These constitute the Naxalite following. In the process, they have also indulged in unpardonable cruelty and indiscriminate killings of land owners by way of vendatta. They have been frustrated by their long and what might have seemed to them an interminable wait. They have lost their faith in the system's ability to deliver the goods and have willy-nilly come to believe that what they thought was justice would not come by itself unless they wrested it from an unresponsive and unwilling system. If only the development programmes had been carried out honestly and without misuse of funds, and if the benefits of the programmes had reached the beneficiaries for whom they were intended, the situation would not have gone the way it has. Even now if justice could be done, 90% of the fence sitters would go along with the Government and to that extent the nature and scope of violence that has been erupting over the last few years would be minimised.

The left wing extremists formed the Bihar Pradesh Kisan Sabha in 1978 and secured a sizeable hold among the landless agricultural labour, who belonged to the Harijan and other backward communities. Pockets of their concentration have been limited to the districts of Patna, Rohtas, Bhojpur, Nalanda and Gaya. On October 4, 1985 the Daman Virodhi Jan Sangarsh Morcha (an organisation to oppose atrocities on people), a front of ten like-minded Kisan organisations of pro-extremist persuasion, staged a massive rally (50,000) at Jahanabagh in Gaya district. The demands of the agitators were, implementation of the Minimum Wages Act, exemption from land revenue, and above all, with-drawal of task forces deployed in the area purportedly to flush out the extremists.

Problems of Bihar which have remained unresolved over the years have repeatedly resulted in grave tragedies. The latest massacre of 44 Thakurs by the Yadvas in Aurangabad district in the last week of May, 1987 was probably the worst in a chain of such killings. This was a sample of what one can expect when agrarian grievances get an infusion of caste conflict. Yet nothing seems to be getting done to reform the institutions such as the police on whose proper, timely and effective functioning depends the peace of any place and more so in a state like Bihar.

References

1. Francine R. Frankel: "Caste, Land and Dominance in Bihar: Breakdown of the Brahminical Social Order" (Quoted from Bihar Gazetteer, Monghyr district).
2. IBID. Francine R. frankel.
3. Study by Bureau of Police Research and Development (1979).
4. Nirmal Sen Gupta: "Agrarian Movements in Bihar" from the book: Agrarian Movements in India – Studies of the 20th Century Bihar.
5. Anand Chakrabarti: "The unfinished struggle of Santhal Bataidars in Purnea district (Bihar) – 1942-1983" in the Economic and Political Weekly – Dt. 25th October, 1986.
6. Agenda papers for the Conference of Revenue Secretaries and Revenue Ministers – Dt. 24th and 25th November, 1986.

CHAPTER 7

LAND REFORMS IN UTTAR PRADESH

Prof. Imtiaz Ahmed and N.C. Saxena had written a paper[1] on: "Caste, Land and Political Power in Uttar Pradesh" in 1984. In the following paragraphs I have drawn on that paper as on my own discusions with the officials of the State Government among others.

There was a time lag of thrre years between the passing of the zamindari abolition Act in 1952 and its implementation which began in 1955. Those who were close to the power elite knew about the impending law much before it was enacted. Many of the land owners made the necessary adjustments and transfers before the law was implemented. Tampering with land records was widely reported. The village level revenue functionaries played a very crucial role in manipulating the records which enabled the land owners to transfer their lands as it suited them. Benami transfers in the name of relatives and friends were freely resorted to. In the name of promoting religious institutions, charitable trusts and educational institutions, large chunks of land were set apart, since the land shown as belonging to such institutions did not attract the provisions of the ceiling prescribed in the law. Unscrupulous land owners availed of this provision to get exemption for the excess land that they still had with them.

The maintenance of land records in Uttar Pradesh, though better than in Bihar, still left serious lacunae. The important functionaries in the Government are very displeased about this state of affairs which apart from being responsible for tortuous litigations has also generated violence between contending factions in the villages. This problem has been further compounded by the institution of Lekha Pal who has taken the place of the Patwari, which post was a hereditary office with its built-in social sanctions. The Lekhapal who has succeeded to this vital office is an appointee of the Government. He enjoys enormous powers and can make or ruin the landowners by what he chooses to interpolate into the records. A dishonest Lekha Pal in collusion with a caste-conscious elected Pradhan can sow the seeds of a great deal of violence in the rural area; there has in fact been enough evidence of it. Further, failure to make timely entries of mutations have created long term problems.

According to a senior Police Officer, in Uttar Pradesh at least 40% of the block Pramukhs elected have a doubtful record of integrity. These elections have generated considerable violence and left behind a trail of bitterness which lingers and erupts again into serious violence between the factions at every opportunity The mafias contribute the money and muscle power.

The Revenue Department functionaries are also responsible for law and order, and their pre-occupation with law and order duties stands in the way of accurate and timely maintenance of land records, which in turn leads to violence. There have been mass murders because of land dispute. In the absence of pillars, the boundaries are vague and demaractions have to be done on the basis of maps. This takes time and it requires the willing co-operation of the Revenue officials at the local level. Often these are not forthcoming.

In Uttar Pradesh the Brahmins constitute 9.2% and the Thakurs 7.2% of the population. Brahmins and Thakurs who constitute 16% of the population corner more than 50% of the political offices. Land Reforms measures did benefit the intermediate castes which make 42% of the population. They have, however, not been able to challenge the supremacy of the centuries old proprietory castes namely, the Brahmins and the Thakurs. The Scheduled Castes contstitute 21% and the Muslims 15% of the population. Only in the hills, the Thakurs constitute more than 50% of the population. Nowhere else, any single caste constitutes more than 25% of a district's population. Thus an important feature of the districts of Uttar Pradesh is their multi-caste character.[2]

Of the 12 lakh acres of land which have been distributed in the last ten years since 1974, 50% has gone to the Scheduled Castes households. They have derived similar benefits in the distribution of house-sites. By an amendment of the Land Reforms Act, 1973 the Scheduled Castes agricultural labour households are given the highest priority in the distribution of surplus land and house sites. In terms of higher education and employment however, the lower half of this group have not been able to avail of these benefits, largely because of the cornering of the benefits by an elite group from among the Scheduled Castes themselves.

According to the study of N.C. Saxena and Imtiaz Ahmed, the Rajputs owned a greater area under proprietory rights than under cultivation rights. This was true also for Banias, Kayasthas and the Muslims. As against this, the Brahmins cultivated more land in many districts rather than rest merely on proprietory rights. The result was that the land reforms affected the Muslims, Banias, Kaysthas and the Thakurs adversely as they stood to lose more land as a result of the tenurial reforms than Brahmins who stood to gain by way of ownership because of the Zamindari abolition. The intermediate castes composed of the Ahirs, Jats, Khurmis, Lodhas, and Gujars, actually cultivated about half of the total land and to that extent benefited by the land reforms. They were also considered good cultivators compared to the upper castes who shied away from manual labour.

According to the 1952 Zamindari Abolition Act, the

Zamindars were allowed to retain their sardari and Khudkasht (self-cultivated) land. Over a period of time, because of the control exercised by the Zamindars on the bureaucracy, a good deal of land was added under this category to the ownership of Zamindars. As mentioned earlier, though the Act itself was passed in 1952 its implementation began only in 1955. The result was that Patwaris falsified land records extensively.

The progress of land reforms in Uttar Pradesh can be gauged from the following figures: 45.31 lakh householders with land upto one acre owned a total of 9.23 lakh acres in 1953-1954. The same category of households owning upto one acre increased to 86.26 lakh households in 1971-1972 owning a total of 16.60 lakh acres. The number of households owning one to 2.5 acres was 23.23 lakh in 1953-1954, owning a total area of 39.39 lakh acres. The corresponding figures for 1971-1972 were 33.38 lakh households owning a total area of 56 lakh acres. Households owning 2.5 to 10 acres of land was 37.28 lakh in 1953-1954 owning a total of 188.26 lkah acres. The corresponding figures for 1971-1972 were 44.15 lakh households owning 213.50 lakh acres. The number of households owning land between 10 to 25 acres was 8.37 lakh in 1953-1954 owning a total area of 151.90 lakh acres. The corresponding figures for 1971-1972 were 6.61 lakh households owning 95 lakh acres. The number of households owning more than 25 acres in 1971-1972 was 72,000 who owned a total of 24.14 lakh acres (These figures are from the National Sample Survey 8th and 26th round quoted by N.C. Saxena). "70% of the rural households in Uttar Pradesh owned less than 2.5 and 5 acres. Uttar Pradesh is a state of tiny holdings."[2]

As against their share of 21% of the total population, the Scheduled Castes households operate on 9.5% of land. Percentage of arca of land holdings upto 5 acres owned by Scheduled Castes is 68.9 of the total area held by them. Of those who operate on large area of 25 acres and above, only 3% belong to Scheduled Castes.

As estimated, the State should have had 5.62 lakh acres surplus land under the Ceiling Act. But the estimate given by the State Government on 1-1-1984 was only 2.94 lakh acres. This gives an idea of the extent of evasion. According to the figures furnished by the State Government it had distributed all the available surplus land by May, 1985. However, 5,327 cases involving 1.445 lakh acres were pending in various courts. In effect, it means that nearly 50% of the surplus land intended for distribution under the Ceiling Act was the subject of litigation. The estimated surplus was only about half of what it should really have been.

Leasing out land is specifically banned in Uttar Pradesh. Law is, however, silent on share-oroppers. This silence was deliberate and calculated. But there are administrative instructions to the field officers forbidding them to record the names of sub-tenants or share-croppers in the land records. According to the 26th National Sample Survey, the total number of households leasing in land in Uttar Pradesh was about 3.5 million out of which 3.4 million owned less than 5 acres. They are entirely at the mercy of land owners, have no security of tenure and their names are also not recorded in the Revenue registers. The National Sample Survey figures under this head are reported to be erring on the lower side and the actual number of share croppers and sub-tenants is estimated at about 5 million. According to the study by N.C. Saxena and Imtiaz Ahmed, restrictions on leasing out of land has broguht in share-cropping system through the back-door, driving the sub-tenancy underground. According to a survey conducted in 1980-1981, the proportion of absentee landlords was highest south of the Jamuna in the most fertile districts. In the eastern districts, this phenomenon is found on a much smaller scale, south of the Jamuna also happens to be the area which is most infested with dacoits.

The extent to which the land reforms have been allowed to be implemented in the spirit in which they were conceived in Uttar Pradesh has been determined by a combination of factors such as the class composition of the MLAs and the Ministers, the orientation of the bureaucracy and the extent of pressure from below exerted by the potential beneficiaries on the politicians and the administrators. In the first three assembly elections, according to one study by Mayer in 1969 (quoted by N.C. Saxena, and Imtiaz Ahmed) 30% of the MLAs came from the family of Zamindars and Taluqdars and 43% from the ranks of cultivators with proprietory rights. Only 24% had non-agricultural background.

The cultivated areas in Tarai of Nainital district was in the possession of the tribals till 1950. Under a scheme of colonisation, huge pieces of land extending from 100 to 5,000 acres were given on lease to refugees from the Punjab and retired military and civil officers. The scheme benefited mostly the Sikhs who came from Pakistan. Gradually these big land owners started encroaching and began to occupy the tribal lands also. Sensing the danger inherent in such a situation, the State Government passed a law declaring further transfer of land from the Tribals to non-Tribals unlawful. The transfers effected till 1969 amounting to about 1,50,000 acres were regularised. In spite of the ligislation, illegal transfer and occupancy of land continued either through physical force or through payment of a paltry sum of about Rs. 500 per acre of land which would have cost several thousands. In all such cases, the Revenus records continue to show the ownership of Tribals over the land because of the restrictions imposed by the Act of 1969. About 15,000 acres are reported to have changed hands under this category after the legislation. In an effort to help the Tribals who were the victims of the greed and high-handedness of the large land owners, the Revenue Secretary proposed that the land so acquired by the land owners should be taken back by the Assistant Collectors suo moto, and he should be authorised to restore the lands to the original Tribal owners using force where necessary. It was also provided that wherever any person after being so evicted from such land by the assistant Collector should re-occupy the land or part thereof without any lawful authority, he should be punished with imprisonment for a term which may extend to three years, with a minimum six months, and in addition a fine. Offences punishable under this amendment were to be cognizable and non-bailable. An ordinance to this effect was issued in June, 1981. "The District administration was not keen to implement this ordinance............ in the meantime representatives of non-Tribals met the Central Cabinet Ministers and talked of harassment to minorities. There was a spate of letters from the Ministers and Farmers Association of Punjab. The Uttar Pradesh Government was accused of making things difficult for the central and Punjab Governments which were trying to solve the Sikh problems."[2] Even though additional police reinforcements were placed at their disposal, the Nainital district authorities kept postponing physical eviction of the non-tribals on various pretexts. "The informal forces working on the district officers were stronger than formal orders of the Gvoernment."[2] In spite of the insistence of the Revenue Secretary on the implementation of the ordinance which was converted into an Act, not a single acre of land had been transferred to the Tribals in the three years preceeding 1984. The only outcome had been the transfer of the Revenue Secretary in 1981.

In yet another instance where the interests of the poor cultivators were involved it was proposed that those who take possession of the land allotted to the agricultural labourers from the Gaon Sabha land should be criminally prosecuted. Though the proposal was accepted by the Cabinet, till 1983 only 158 prosecutions had been filed, none of which resulted in conviction. Here again the culprits who would have had to be prosecuted and would have to be relieved of the adverse possessions were the more influential sections of the landed class; hence the lukewarm implementation of the Government's decisions.

The above instances deserve to be viewed in the context of yet another Government order in which the targets were the poor people. According to a decision taken in 1978, it was proposed to oust agricultural labourers from those of the Gaon Sabha lands where permanent cultivation was not possible or which were being used by the entire village community as pasture or grazing land. "Within six months more than 60,000 cases were filed in the revenue courts against the rural poor. The Government got alarmed at the high number of conviction it would have led to and, therefore, stayed further action. Finally in 1981, the allotment was regularised and the conviction proceedings were abated."[2]

If implemented correctly and strictly the land reforms in Uttar Pradesh are bound to disturb the existing political and economic structures. Undestandably, therefore, those who stand to lose their political leverage arising out of their economic affluence are the ones who resist the strict implementation of the land reforms. They have the money power and with it goes the political power. In Uttar Pradesh and Bihar, they virtually dominate all political parties except the leftist parties. S.P. Gupta, who served in several capacities in Uttar Pradesh before retiring from the Indian Administrative Services, has observed: "The Uttar Pradesh imposition of ceiling on land Holding Act, 1960 was amended eight times between 1961 and 1976....... In our politico-Administrative culture the field revenue officials like other field officials, are completely demoralised (even if not corrupt) and are at the mercy of locally influential people (mostly large land holders). The report of the Uttar Pradesh Commission on District level Administration of August, 1986 concludes that the cases under the Uttar Pradesh imposition of Ceiling on Land continue to linger on for years; the revenue staff at the lower level is hand in glove with large land holders. In some instances the Ceiling Act cases are pending for over a decade. In many cases possession of the allottees is on paper only...... Unless the deprived sections of society organise themselves and wage a relentless war agaisnt delays, corruption, evasion and social and economic injustice, the administration including the Courts will continue to be manoeuvred by those who wield money and muscle power."[3]

References

1. Prof. Imtiaz Ahmed and N.C. Saxena : "Caste, Land and Political Power in Uttar Pradesh" (1984).
2. IBID.
3. S.P. Gupta : "Uttar Pradesh Land Reforms" in Indian Express, a national daily, Dt. 5th November, 18 1986.

CHAPTER 8

LAND REFORMS IN GUJARAT

According to Ganshyam Shah[1] : On the first day of the formation of Saurashtra State in April, 1948, the new Government dominated by Vanias and Brahmins granted occupancy rights to the cultivators without compensatory payment. For the first time, the cultivators got the right of transferring and inheriting land. The result of the land reforms in Saurashtra in the wake of independence led to one of the most even distribution of land holdings of any region in India. Though some of the Girasdars who were the owners of land launched agitations aginst the reforms and some of them resorted to dacoities, the stern handling of the problems by the State led to the collapse of the revolt.

Unlike the Girasdari Act of Saurashtra, the tenancy act was not rigorously implemented in Gujarat. This is partly because the Pattidars, commonly known as Patels, Vanias and Brahmin landowners, who would have been adversely affected by the Act, dominated the Congress party and the administration. At the same time, the Act did not fail altogether either. Dr. Ganshyam Shah quotes M.B. Desai who had carried out a sample survey in 65 villages thus: "About half the area previously under tenancy passed into the ownership of the respective erstwhile tenants. About 12% of the land held by 9% tenants continued under recognised tenancy. A little over 2% of the land of tenants slipped from them in default of payment of compensation amount. The rest were cases in which the tenants either denied their tenancy, surrendered the land to the land owners, or kept away from the hearings of the tribunal and, therefore, missed of their own volition to be owners of the land they cultivated on lease." Thus a sizeable tenancy escaped ownership under tenancy abolition. The net result of the land reform has been that most of the tenants belonging to the lower castes or Scheduled Castes did not have the courage to avail of the provisions of acquiring ownership as it would have meant standing up and claiming their rights from the upper castes. For this, they were not prepared. They, therefore, surrendered their tenancy.

Concealed tenancy in different forms continued. The land ceiling law which was passed in 1960 and which was later amended in 1974 to lower the ceiling has remained largely on paper. Only 43,721 acreas of land of inferior quality was surrendered. "The Government rejected even the simple suggestion of forming a watchdog committee to observe the implementation of the Ceiling Act. Nor did the Government take any other steps to gear up the adminsitrative machinery to implement the Act. The farmers took a pledge in public that surplus land would not be surrendered to the Government for distribution among the landless under the land Ceiling Act."[2] The land reforms, though they led to redistribution of land to some extent, have not substantially changed the land relationships in terms of caste or class.

There are about 19 unions of agricultural labourers in rural Gujarat with membership of less than one lakh which is barely 4% of the total number of agricultural workers. The majority of them are not organised for collective bargaining. They display occasionally a degree of militancy and resort to stoppage of work demanding higher wages or village common land for house-sites or for grazing their cattle or protesting against land owners sexually assaulting their women folk.

The landed classes have a system of employing watchmen called "Rakha' to protect their crops. There are a number of instances of violence by Rakhas against labourers. Rakhas are usually people from outside the area selected for their muscle power.

Though the Minimum Wages Act had been revised in 1982 raising wages from Rs. 5.50 to Rs. 11/- per day, agricultural labourers rarely get their prescribed wages, except in Saurashtra. The Labour Officers appointed to enforce the law hardly ever enforce it. They never visit the villages. They expect the labourers to visit their offices and report about lower wages. Under the Act, the farmers are expected to keep records of the wages paid; but such records are hardly ever maintained. The amount of fine collected by the Courts from the land owners for their failure to pay minimum wages and for the non-maintenance of stipulated records in 1981, 1982, 1983 were Rs. 31,785/-; Rs. 82,897/- and Rs. 2.06 lakh respectively. That the trend is towards non-conformity with the legal stipulation is evident from this.

In the light of the foregoing the conclusion that emerges is that Gujarat like Uttar Pradesh and Bihar has within itself considerable volume of exploitative violence induged in by the vested interests.

References

1. Dr. Ganshyam Shah : "Caste Sentiments, Class formation and dominance in Gujarat" (1984).
2. IBID

CHAPTER 9

LAND REFORMS IN WEST BENGAL

Rural unrest connected with land reform started appearing in West Bengal around 1967. It started as a protest by the peasants against the non-implementation of the land Ceiling Act. The peasants under the newly emerging Naxalite leadership started occupying the land vested in the State on the ground that the lands did not belong to the landholders who continued to claim it even though it was in excess of what they had been allowed under the Ceiling Act. They demanded that such of the land which in effect belonged to the people be distributed among the landless. The then Government of West Bengal decided to constitute Police Station level Committees for overseeing the distribution of vested lands. The membership of these Committees was composed of representatives of the various political parties as also the Government. The Committees were to decide on the allotment of surplus land among the landless on the spot after examining the claims on their merits. The Committee work was followed by spot orders by the Minister concerned. The Government issued instructions that in all the disputes between the tenants and the land owners, the Police would extend their support to the tenants. This system of allotment of vested land worked very well till 1969 when it received a setback following the introduction of the President's rule in the State. This gave an impetus to the Naxalite movement with all its violence and the numerous murders in cold blood, all of which have since become a part of the unforgettable and gory history of West Bengal during that period.

The bulk of the rural poor in West Bengal are sharecroppers and landless labourers. Tenancy in the past had been based largely on informal arrangements. As a consequence, laws designed to reduce the amount of the crop that the share-cropper had to give to the land owner, and laws to improve the security of tenure had been operationally ineffective. To alter this situation, the Communist Party (Marxist) regime had undertaken a concerted effort to legally register the share croppers' names in the hope that this would improve their income and provide them greater security.

One of the early acts of the CPM Government was to introduce The Land Reform Amendment Bill in 1977. This Bill introduced a few important safeguards which taken together were designed to provide a definite sense of security to the tenants. The Bill placed the onus of proving that a man is not a share cropper on the landowners. This protected the tenant farmers from arbitrary eviction. "Personal cultivation" was defined to exclude cultivation by servants or hired labourers. Failure to issue receipts to share croppers was made a cognizable offence. The Amendment also sought to remove absentee landlordism and the related large scale holdings by non-agriculturists. These steps gave teeth to the implementation of the land reforms in West Bengal, a characteristic all of its own and which has contributed significantly to defusing tensions and violence arising out of possible conflicts over land in the countryside. This is in such sharp contrast to the situation obtaining in Bihar and Uttar Pradesh.

Mr. Atul Kohli has dealt with in his paper[1] the special steps taken by the Communist Party (Marxist) in West Bengal with regard to the land laws. The Government undertook a special drive called 'Operation Barga, which facilitated rapid registration of share croppers. "Teams of bureaucrats and/or party members, activists and Kisan Sabha members were sent out to the countryside to announce the laws and to register the share croppers on the spot. The operation has had considerable success. While over the previous three decades, fewer than 60,000 share croppers were registered in the areas where the CPM is now operating, in its first five years the CPM succeeded in registering over 1.2 million. Compared to the past performances of Congress and other regimes in the area, the CPM's success is spectacular."[2] According to the agenda papers of the Revenue Ministers' Conference held in November, 1986 till the end of 1985 a total of 1.3 million share-croppers had been registered. The estimated number of share-cropping families is about 1.5 million.

The share-croppers who stood to benefit from the amended laws constituted the sheet anchor of the CPM party cadres in the rural areas. The CPM has also concentrated on providing extra employment in the rural areas by setting up employment generating schemes. It has also seen to the effective enforcement of the minimum wages. "As the political fortunes of the CPM are closely tied to the success of such distributive schemes, sustained pressure through party has minimised the typical problems of corruption and maladministration."[2]

The CPM Government of West Bengal allowed political parties to compete for local Government positions. The result was that 98% of the seats at the district level 74% at the block level and 67% at the village level were captured by the CPM candidates in 1979. The 1983 Panchayat elections were a near-repeat performance. "The CPM regime along with newly created local governments thus represents two interlinked patterns of political change: an organisational penetration by the 'centre' into the 'periphery' and a simultaneous shift in the class basis of institutional power."[2]

The CPM has demonstrated that the implementation of land reforms is a feasible proposition, given the political will to ensure that vested interests do not impede the progress of the reforms. The policies of CPM generate their own brand of violence in the course of their conflict with what they consider as their class enemies. But looking merely at the limited problem of the economically marginalised peasantry, the manner in which the CPM brought about the redistribution of land among the peasantry with little or no violence carries its own political message.

References

1. Atul Kohli : "From Elite Radicatism to Democratic Consolidation : The rise of Reform communism in West Bengal" (1984).
2. IBID

PART IV

Chapter 10

CASTE CONFLICT AND AGRARIAN VIOLENCE IN BIHAR

An effort will be made in this part to illustrate with the help of specific cases, the types, and the intensity of violence that have characterised the rural areas of Bihar and parts of Uttar Pradesh, Maharashtra and Gujarat during the last decade. In the course of this study, the experiences of Karnataka and West Bengal have been alluded to with a view to highlighting how politics when employed as an instrument of change, social change can be effected without violence as a necesary concomitant.

This is not intended to be a catalogue of violent incidents. Much less does this account give details of incidents involving violence, in the various states. This is an attempt to analyse a few of the several causative factors that have contributed to violence, and to the extent possible identify such of the factors as would lend themselves to a 'therapeutic' effort. I have focussed on those areas where with proper planning of the many programmes in the context of the institutional capability of the delivery system, it should have been possible to avert violence which was otherwise to be expected.

The mindless killings in the several incidents referred to here have just become mere meaningless statistics in the climbing graph of devastated homes. One does not have to labour the point that the violence in the instances cited, both with regard to their intensity and variety are largely the outcome of the socio-economic changes in the country during the last decade. We cannot wait for a change in human nature for achieving semblance of peace and harmony in a society under change. This has to be brought about by the innovation and even radical changes in institutions. If there is one truth that has been consecrated by history, it is that a country can achieve nothing if its institutional infrastructure is corrupt, partisan, ineffective and inefficient. Those who prevent creation of institutions or subvert them, however insidiously, for personal, party of caste interests, contribute to the volume of violence in our society, each in his own self-serving ways.

Many of the issues which eventually ended in violence have begun as first-time problems. The existing institutions were not designed to cope with nor have they been suitably innovated or the required number of appropriate new ones created, and strategically located, to meet the changes in the political and socio-economic conditions which characterise independent India.

One aspect of violence in Bihar which needs to be emphasized is that a large number of people have come to occupy positions of eminence in the economic and political life of the State whose upward mobility from the lowest rung was facilitated by violence. Violence in Bihar has been receiving a social acceptability as an inevitable concomitant of growth of political and economic power. Otherwise it is not possible to explain why individuals who had used muscle power came to occupy positions of power in the socio-economic and political life of the State. These centres of power became an invitation to others waiting in the wings with the same "qualifications" as the successful wielders of economic and political power. If anything, they are practitioners of a more sophisticated form of violence.

Violence by the economically strong against the weaker sections has become endemic in Bihar. The labourers in Karghar block of Rohtas district had organized a strike in March, 1977 to secure minimum wages. This provoked the landholders to attack the Harijans in their residential areas in which three labourers were shot and burnt alive in a haystack. In Gopalpur also the labourers who had struck work demanding minimum wages were attacked by the landholders in June, 1977. Many of them were injured and their women molested. On 19th June, 1977 in Patahada in Bhagalpur district, 36 men and women from among the labourers were confined to a school building and brutally assaulted. In Bharampura, 4 share-croppers were killed by the landholders for demanding occupancy rights on October 27, 1977. In all these incidents it was openly alleged that the landholders enjoyed the tacit backing of the local police chief who allegedly belonged to one of their castes.

The shameful Belchi incident in 1978 in which 11 Harijans were burnt alive was the upshot of a long standing feud between Kurmi landholders and the Scheduled Castes agricultural labourers over the payment of the minimum wages and extraction of forced labour. The entire crime was well-planned and organised. It was alleged that there was a tacit understanding between the local police and the landholders. It was not a sudden eruption. Economic issues of a long standing nature were involved. Evidently nothing was done at the administrative level to sort out the differences which could have prevented this ghastly incident. Presumably the existing administrative institutional safeguards are either unsuited or inadequate to meet the purpose.

That a distinct re-orientation is required on the part of the police in the handling of cases of atrocities against the Harijans is proved by the manner in which they had handled some of the cases in Bihar. In a case reported from Monghyr district in 1979, a village cobbler was killed by some Rajputs in collusion with the police and the Home Guards. This incident which was the outcome of a long standing land dispute was inquired into by the District Magistrate. He came to the conclusion that the story as reported by the Police Sub-Inspector of the area was false.

The Scheduled Caste individual was the aggrieved party and needed to be protected, which was not done which resulted in his death.

In another case reported from village Samhanta in Rohtas district of Bihar in June, 1979, four Harijans were killed by some Rajputs. The underlying cause was again land dispute which had been going on for about ten years. The Commissioner for Scheduled Castes had this inquired into by a senior Police Officer who came to the conclusion that the Sub-Inspector in charge of this area was in collusion with the local Rajput landowners and they were responsible for the killing of the four Harijans. The local Police had tried to give the incident the colour of an encounter with dacoits resulting in the death of four persons which was totally false. The concerned Police officials were later ordered to be prosecuted.

The Harijan locality of Pipra village in Patna district was invaded by the Kurmi land owners on 26th February, 1980. The invaders, numbering about 200 were armed with guns. They were alleged to have set fire to 27 houses of Harijans and shot the people, looted their property and burnt alive their cattle. It has been reported that the assailants indulged in unbelievable brutality like throwing a three-year-old child into the fire. In all, 14 Harijans lay dead which included 5 women, 3 adults and 6 children. Though the incident stretched over 6 hours, the Police from the nearest Police Station, which was only 3 kilometres away from the scene of the tragedy, did not reach the spot till after thc whole tragedy was over. The Kurmis in this case were avenging the murder of one Bola Singh by the Naxalities who were organising the Harijans of this area to resist the tyranny of the Kurmi landholders.

Considering the manner in which the Police behave on all such occasions, it is difficult to disbelieve the allegations made by the weaker sections that the Police is quite often in collusion with the upper and intermediate caste landowners. In Bihar, most of the armed Police posted in the rural areas to supplement the local Police and patrol the areas of Naxalite influence live in the. Estate (Katcheries) of the landholders and avail of their hospitality, as there is no provision for independent accomodation in rural areas for Police reinforcements. These extra Police detachments have to stay over long periods when they develop links with the landholders. To expect them thereafter to act against the interests of the landholders is just not possible. Here is an aspect of policing in which the fall-out from the socio-economic changes that have been taking place following the land reforms and the other changes should have been taken into consideration. But the Police system continues to function in much the same way as it was several decades prior to Independence, with marginal changes if at all.

In a State where caste conflict is endemic and the society stands hopelessly divided on caste lines, the composition of the Police force which has a cruicial role to play in resolving the conflicts is a very important factor. The representation of the weaker sections in the Police force has to be visibly improved at the operational level. Not much attention was paid in the past to this aspect of caste composition of police force.

Rafiq Khan and Shiv Swarat Singh[1], two scholars of the Gandhian Institute of Studies, Varanasi, did a case study of the atrocities on Harijans with special reference to the Bhishrampur village in Dinara block of Rohtas district in Bihar (1978). According to them; "So much insecurity has come to dominate the village on account of inefficient administration that possessing some illegal arms to protect oneself from robbers is regarded as a necessity....... Policemen are never tired of narrating dacoits and murderers who are regularly patronised by this or that leader, many of whom are important men in the Gvoernment. The illegal arms are so widespread....... It is widely believed by non-Harijan castes that a large number of Harijan households are fully equipped with guns and grenades. The Harijans on the other hand told us that every family in the Kurmi caste has guns, in some cases with licence and in some without."

Parasbhiga village of Jehanabad sub-division of Gaya district was the scene of one of the worst massacres resulting from caste conflicts. This happened in February, 1980. This village was invaded by the Bumihars and the houses of the Harijans were set on fire. When the inmates tried to escape, they were shot and pushed back in the flame. In all, 12 live were lost. This was an act of revenge by the Bumihars for the suspected involvement of a member of a shepherd family of the village in the murder of one of the Bumihar landowners in October, 1979.

There have been allegations of collusion between the Police and the upper caste Bumihars who were responsible for the massacre at Parasbhiga. "The role of the administration, it is reported, has been adversely commented upon by the one-man commission under Mr. M.K. Prashad, Revenue Member, appointed by the Government to go into this incident. It is significant that this report was not placed on the table of the Bihar Assembly. Some Members of Legislative Assembly told this author that it contained incriminating information regarding the behaviour of the administration and the politicians."[2]

On April 3, 1982 six persons were killed in the Police firing in Baluha in Rajnagar block of Madhubani district of Bihar. Two more persons were reportedly beaten to death, though their names did not figure in the official list. This was a sequel to the conflicts between Harijans and backward caste peasants on the one side and upper caste landowners on the other. The peasants had demanded wage increase as stipulated under the law which was conceded but was not given effect to by the landowners. The tension escalated gradually over certain other incidents till it resulted in Police firing. The Baluha outrage was in a sense an instance of the landowner-police response to the peasant labour movement building up in Bihar. This is one more instance in which the police had allegedly sided with the vested interests.

The widening gap between the Government programmes and their implementation needs to be viewed in the context of the potential for violence that it holds. Unless the administrative agencies function impartially, the vested interests will regard what in fact has accrued to them by acting in their exploitative capacity as legitimate part of their privileges.

An operation Black Panther was launched in March, 1985 agaisnt kidnappings for ransom, which had been plaguing West Champaran for six years. The dacoits who indulged in this crime had reportedly links with big landowners or influential leaders of West Champaran. During this operation, one of the outlaws was killed in the house of a close relative of a political leader, while another dacoit was arrested from the house of an M.L.A. According to one version, the former musclemen of landowners took to crime following land reforms. These musclemen started helping sugarcane cultivators to sell their produce and also made advance payment on behalf of the big traders at a considerable discount. Thus a nexus developed between the big cultivators, rich traders and the musclemen. Since the musclemen knew how much money these traders and cultivators had, they thought of the idea of kidnapping. According to the official figures, only 5 kidnapping cases were registered in 1981 but the number rose to 16 in 1982, 48 in 1983 and 83 in 1984. Till June of 1985 there had been 25 cases.

On 22nd August, 1984 about 150 people belonging to the Bhumihar community looted and burnt the huts built on Government land by 100 Harijan families in village Ambari of Monghyr district. Many of the Harijans were beaten up. According to the district Magistrate of Monghyr, the Bumihars who committed this atrocity on the Harijans were motivated by a desire to appropriate the land belonging to the Government. Some of the important facts brought out from a study of this case in its details are:

First, the Revenue Circle Officer who played the most crucial role in getting the land allotted to the Bhumihar, knowing well that about 100 Harijan families were settled on the plot, was himelf a Harijan. The District Magistrate held him primarily responsible for the entire series of events along with the other higher functionaries. Apparently he and others had been bribed.

Second, the State officials far from playing an objective role, were working in collusion with the vested interests and against the weaker sections.

The Diara lands which are usually very fertile and the size and shape of which vary continuously because of the changing course of the river, has no fixed land marks and is constantly under dispute. Establishing one's right on such land depends largely on muscle and money power. There are reportedly about 50 to 60 gangs operating in the Diara area of Monghyr district, who are notorious for their acts of extreme violence. In one such incident, on 11th November, 1985 about a thousand armed men belonging to the Yadav community swooped on the village Lakshmipur and opened fire on Binds with whom the Yadavs had dispute over a piece of land. The Yadavs are reported to have killed 12 persons; gangraped their women and set fire to more than 200 houses. Though the Binds had been voicing their fear of impending attack on them even 15 days before the incident, no action was taken by the authorities. Indifference on the part of the Police on the pretext of certain legal niceties is a recurring source of violence in the rural areas generally. This is an area where appropriate institutional innovation has not been forthcoming in spite of the loss of so many innocent lives.

In Kapri Police Station of Jehanabad district two Harijans were killed by a group of Bhumihars on 19th October, 1985 in village Saibali. This incident was a sequel to some land being cultivated by the Harijans which was sought to be taken over by the upper castes. Subsequently, the District Magistrate allotted the land to the Harijan families. This tragedy could well have been averted if action by the authorities had been initiated earlier, though the execuse for not taking action earlier was that the law did not provide for taking action unless there was manifest violence of a given degree. This is another instance of the laws enacted about a hundred years ago being out of tune with the requirements of the times.

On 5th December, 1984, 10 out of 13 Kurmis who were sleeping in a house in village Dhularpur of Punpun area of Patna district were shot dead. Many of those who were killed were standing trial on charge of murder and were on bail. According to the investigation by the police, it was suspected that this massacre was done by some persons from Scheduled Castes or their sympathisers as some of those killed were members of the Bhumi Sena, an armed wing of the Kurmi landowners, notorious for atrocities on the Harijans in the area.

The Bhumi Sena is primarily an organisation of Kurmis belonging to Gaya, Patna and Nalanda districts. The Bhumi Sena is accused of raising a tax of Rs. 2.50 per bigha per year from the landowners and from every Government servant a sum of Rs. 2/- a year. It has also been reported by the Government agencies that as its influence increased, it also started committing crimes. It has been accused of levying a toll even from people who were not in need of its assistance. Those who fail to pay the levy are harassed in several ways. One of these is to declare them as 'Naxalites'. The people including some of the Kurmis themselves are most unhappy with the activities of this Sena. It is reported to have a fund of Rs. 2.5 to Rs. 3 lakhs. It has no political affiliations.

The Lal Sena of the Red Army has some ideological content behind its origin and operations, unlike the other Senas which are the creation of landed interests, as an expedient for subserving caste or group interests. The Lal Sena does not belong to any caste group unlike the Kuwar Sena which represents Thakurs, the Brahma Rishi Sena which represents the Bhumihars, the Lohrik Sena which represents the Yadavs and the Bhumi Sena which represents the Kurmis. The Lal Sena has got a wider popular base because it is not caste-oriented. It had its origin initially in Bhojpur in 1974 when it came into conflict with the police in which several of them were killed. The Lal Sena has since spread to Patna, Gaya and Nalanda. It has amongst its members youths in the age group of 18 to 30. Its leadership is often in the hands of the upper castes.

According to the police sources, in the initial stages, the Yadavs who used to join the Lal Sena in large numbers used to commit several crimes which was not approved by the leaders of the Lal Sena. They, therefore, decided to purge the Lal Sena of such elements. The elements remvoed from the Lal Sena in combination with the better ones among the Yadavs, formed a Sena which came to be known as the Lohrik Sena. One of the aims of the Lohrik Sena is to confront the memebrs of the Lal Sena openly.

A private army calling itself the Lohrik Sena raided four vilalges in Nalanda district on 15th November, 1985 and killed three persons supposed to be members of the Lal Sena, the army of the extremists. The killing was allegedly in retaliation for the murder of a Lohrik Sena member by Lal Sena a day earlier. Two other alleged Nax alites were killed about the same time in Gaya district. The violence in Nalanda and Gaya was a sequel to the disputes over minimum wages for harvesting crops. In the case in which the Lohrik Sena members had gone to a village in

Gaya district and killed certain alleged Naxalites for what they had done earlier, it has been clearly brought out in the official reports that the Station House Officer of one of the police stations of Nalanda district and his staff were seen in the company of the memebrs of the Lohrik Sena. The police officer tried to explain his presence with the Lohrik Sena on the ground that he was there trying to chase the Naxalities. Though the Police Officer acknowledged in the presence of responsible officials that he had seen the members of the Lohrik Sena in possession of arms and also knew that they would commit a crime any time, still he took no steps to seize the weapons from the Lohrik Sena members. The Lohrik Sena members committed the murder of a sixty-year-old man and looted a few houses and relieved some women of their jewellery. The preparation was within the knowledge of the police officer and could have been averted.

These private armies are well organised and well provided with country made guns of various types, most of which are manufactured indigenously in Monghyr district. This district produces fire arms on a commercial scale, almost on the lines of a factory.

It has been alleged that when the labourers assert themselves demanding minimum wages they are dealt with ruthlessly by the police, labelling them as Naxalites. This is in contrast to the indulgence that the members of the Senas other than Lal Sena enjoy at the hands of the law enforcing authorities. A procession of landowners carrying guns, spears and swords with caparisoned elephants was taken out to demonstrate the strength of the Bhumi Sena in 1983. This procession was taken out in spite of prohibitory orders. Slogans were shouted by the processionists which were derogatory of the Lal Sena. One of the slogans was: "Naxalyon Ki Kya Dawai? Che Che Inch deo Bhai" (What is the remedy for the Naxalities? Shorten them by six inches). It implied chopping their heads off.

The distrubing aspect of the activities of the Senas is that even the police finds it expedient to encourage some of these Senas as long as their activities are directed against the Lal Sena which is the armed wing of the Naxalities. This short sighted policy has a dangerous potential. Often what the Senas indulge in are acts of vendetta divorced from idelogical considerations. These actions are explained away by the police on the assumption that the victim or the victims were Naxalities. The fact that the State administration for whatever reason, was not taking steps to contain the activities of these Senas can lead to inferences which may not be complimentary to the State administration. How can any private individual or groups be allowed to act on behalf of the State in an unauthorised way? This is abdication of authority by the State or an acknowledgement that the State's writ does not run in certain areas or that it does not want to interfere in the activities of certain selected groups or individuals. However one looks at it, it is a pathetic commentary both on the political and the administrative authority of the Government. In the latter half of 1986, the State Government is reported to have taken steps to ban these private armies. The impact of this decision remains to be seen.

According to official figures the number of murders in which Naxalities were involved in Bihar was 53 in 1982, 38 in 1983, 28 to 1984, and 28 till the end of September, 1985. The Naxalities are reported to have snatched from the public 4 rifles and 36 guns in 1983, 3 rifles and 7 guns in 1984; 3 rifles and 9 guns till the end of August, 1985. In 1984, the Naxalites snatched 20 rifles from the police and in 1985 till the end of August they had snatched 5 rifles from the police.

The Director General of Police-Bihar in a statement to the Press stated that on April 19, 1986 the police opened fire in the area of Police Station Arwal of Jehanabad subdivision of Gaya district against a crowd of people who were alleged to be Naxalites. They are alleged to have attacked the Superintendent of Police of Jehanabad. In all, 53 rounds were fired, killing 11 alleged Naxalites on the spot and causing injury to 20. Later, 12 of the injured died in the Hospital bringing the death toll to 23. According to the Home Commissioner, this incident could have been averted had the police not been a silent spectator in the beginning allowing more than 500 people to assemble in contravention of the prohibitory orders which had been imposed earlier. The holocaust had its beginning in a land dispute between the Harijans on the one side and a Senior Engineer on the other. The police version has been characterised as slanted by some journalists and also by some Congress legislators who had investigated the incident on the spot.

The ex-Chief Justice of the Delhi High Court, Shri Rajinder Sachar and Lt. Gen Shri S.K. Sinha (Retd.) did an on the spot inquiry of the police firing at Arwal. The land in dispute which reportedly belonged to Rasak had not been entered in the record of rights. The records mentioned that the land had been described as the Bihar Sarkar Anabad. The Home Commissioner told Justice Sachar and Lt. Gen. Sinha (Retd.) that the District magistrate of Gaya, in the initial report to the Government about the firing had observed that the firing at Arwal had been uncontrolled, excessive and without any orders from the Magistrate.

About the Arwal police firing, the one-man Commission that inquired into it came to the conclusion that not only had the police used excessive force but that restraint could have averted deaths. In this, as in several other similar cases, the inference is inescapable that there was a nexus between the police and the vested interests. The recurring incidents which point to such collusion between the administration and the vested interests at various levels against the interests of the weaker sections point to the inevitable conclusion that the Government needs to display greater political will and courage if its credibility in helping the weaker sections of society is not to suffer any further. These are the occasions when the accountability of the police to the people needs to be demonstrated.

There was a report of two armed encounters between private armies of landholders and the Lal Sena of the Naxalites whcih are reported to have left 15 people dead and many injured during the second week of April, 1986. These encounters took place in Gaya and Patna districts, according to the Home Commissioner of Bihar.

According to Times of India dated 2nd May, 1986 the Police chief of Bihar is reported to have admitted in a note prepared by him that the police had been encouraging the private armies of landowners in areas of Naxalite activity in central Bihar. He has been quoted as having recorded that the "Police in these areas had abdicated their normal duties and the tendency among the police functionaries was to encourage the defence groups (the Senas) to organize themselves in order to fight out the Naxalites. This was the very negation of police performance which actually resulted in the rise of different Senas in Bihar".[3]

The caste war in Bihar took yet another toll of ten human lives on 8th July 1986 which included two children and six women in village Kansari under the Jehanabad Police Circle at Arwal. It is astonishing that the police Head Quarters at Patna and Gaya, which are fairly close to the scene of the event became aware of it forty hours after it had occured. This massacre was by way of retaliation by the upper castes aganist the killing of a landholder by a suspected activist of the Mazdoor Kisan Sangram Samiti which usually spearheads the cause of the landless for minimum agricultural wages and generally against oppression and exploitation. It was again alleged in this case as in such cases in the past that the police had colluded with the landholders in the caste war.

In Bhagalpur district, three women agricultural labourers were shot dead by the police on 5th December,

1986. According to a report[4] in the Indian Express dated 8th December, 1986 the tragedy was triggered off by an affluent landholder who had land far in excess of his entitlement under the Ceiling Act. The women were agitating for the recognition of tenancy rights and minimum wages. The police had gone to the village to stop the forcible harvesting of crops.

The ruthless massacre of more than forty members belonging to the Rajput community by the Yadavas on May 29th, 1987, in the villages of Dalalchak and Badhura in Aurangabad district of Bihar was the culmination of a chain of vendetta killings in which the members of both the communities had indulged in on different occasions starting from September 4, 1986. The series of tragedies can be traced to the time when almost two dozen Yadavs who had been tilling the land belonging to the Salupara Math for years as share croppers were forcibly dispossessed by a Rajput to whom the Salupara Math donated the land to escape the impact of the Land Ceiling Act. This forcible dispossession had infuriated the Yadavas who had been looking forward to the time when the land cultivated by them would become theirs consequent on the Ceiling Act. They then became members of an activist group which had been known as Maoist Communist Centre (MCC). The Yadavas fired the first shot when they killed on September 4, 1986, an employee of the Rajput who had dispossessed them of their tilling rights. They also killed another Rajput on 10th September, 1986. The Rajput avenged these deaths on September 20th, 1986 by killing six of the MCC activists in Village Parsadih. As a sequel to this, the MCC activists raided the Village Darmia in Aurangabad district on October 10, 1986 and murdered mercilessly eleven Rajputs whcih included women and children. The Rajput response to this was to gun down seven Yadavas in Cheechani village in April, 1987. It was alleged that while this killing was going on there were about twenty-five armed policemen barely one kilometer away and they did not intervene. In spite of these series of reprisal killings, no meaningful police effort was forthcoming to prevent further violence is borne out by the massacre of Rajputs on May 29th, 1987 in the villages of Dalalchak and Badhura. These series of cruel killings illustrate most insistently the following points:

Land dispute has taken a heavy toll in terms of human lives in Bihar. Next to adult franchise which has a unique place in the evolution of the political institutions of the country, land reforms have been the most important measure introduced in the post-independence period which has had far reaching socio-economic impact on the Indian society. This, in spite of the fact that there is considerable gap between the land reforms envisaged and the reforms actually implemented. Even this process of implementation has been more than painful and has been the largest single source of violence. This could well have been significantly mitigated if the authorities had provided adequate institutional safeguards for containing the fall out from the problems which are in the nature of first time problems. If appropriate institutional back up had been provided to resolve the problems expeditiously, unequivocally and at or near the sources of their origin, this far reaching reform could have been accomplished with much less murderous violence even if not in complete peace. This could well have transformed the rural society as nothing else would have.

These incidents also prove that the so called weaker sections can no longer be taken for granted and oppressed and emasculated socially and/or economically. They have developed their own clout and will fight back if necessary. What is more they as a caste group and in their own right are also capable of indulging in murderous violence against the members of the so called upper castes.

The police system has proved itself incapable of anticipating the course of events with a view to contain the problems before they assume proportions. Each of these violent incidents in such quick succession amply prove the inadequacy and/or the inappropriateness of the police system to absorb the fall out from the changes that are coming over the society.

Some districts in Bihar have also witnessed several forcible harvesting of standing crops belonging to the legitimate land holders, by peasants during March, 1987. The police has been powerless to prevent this trend and these several acts of lawlessness have shown up the criminal justice system in a rather dim light. Such organised instances of defiance of law by people who are not normally treated as criminals pose a serious threat to the concept of the rule of law. If one were to analyse the several facts leading up to the present state of affairs, one cannot miss the point that at some stage in the chain of events, even the vested interests in collusion with political power had themselves failed to abide by the rule of law. Therefore, considering the signs of the times, it would be an act of enlightened self interest on the part of those who are economically stronger to develop a vested interest in the rule of law, as they stand to lose more in the long run in the absence of it. It is high time the authorities in Bihar demonstrated that they have within the system something in the nature of political and administrative will capable of handling the problems of violence, among other things. As of now this seems to be in serious doubt.

An important element in the worsening relationship between Kurmis and the Harijans is sex. The Harijans no longer allow their womenfolk to work in the houses of Kurmis. Asserts Dwarika Ravidas, a Harijan: "We can never have good relations with them. They pay us less, they abuse us, beat up our children, and use our wives, sisters and daughters. It is a life we can never tolerate."[5] The youth among the Harijans who are educated and have jobs with the Government in urban areas would no longer accept or tolerate such exploitation of their women-folk. The Harijans are no longer afraid to speak out and are prepared to stand up against high-handedness. One of them told me: "If we raise our voice for implementation of minimum wages, if we want education for our women, we are termed Naxalites."

While the Harijan continues to suffer a sense of deprivation, he has also gained a new sense of self respect. The right to vote has brought to his doorstep, the high and the mighty in the social hierarchy. But this in turn has also induced a sense of frustration as socially he still feels left out of the mainstream by the untouchability practised agaisnt him. In a sense, his social status which remains where it was centuries ago, does not correspond to his newly acquired political status.

A consensus has begun to emerge among the Scheduled Castes in Bihar on a political strategy to benefit them. The leadership have come to realise the need for a social and economic revolution for bringing about a social revolution apart from benefits of reservation. The leadership is beginning to clamour for new directions in economic policy which will provide employment oriented development projects to benefit small farmers and the landless agricultural labourers.

It would be hasty to conclude that the caste conflict in Bihar or Uttar Pradesh is always in the nature of a direct confrontation between what are traditionally known as upper castes and lower castes. Intracaste group conflict among the backward castes is equally common. There have also been cases of individuals from the upper castes leading the Naxalites whose rank and file primarily consist of the Scheduled Castes.

The continuing uncertainties with regard to land and related matters affecting the weaker sections have provided an ideological base to the left extremists who pass for Naxalites. There are several factions among the leftist groups all of whom however are agreed on their belligerent, hostile and antagonistic attitude towards the land owners who continue to display feudalistic tendencies. In acts of revenge against landowners, they have been guilty of as much cruelty as the landowners themselves.

Uttam Sengupta, who had travelled through most of rural Bihar and written a report in the Calcutta edition of The Telegraph dated 26th October, 1986 has observed that according to official sources the armed units of the CPML (Communist Party of India Marxist Lenist) had actually occupied around 10,000 acres of land. "What is more important however is the Party's claim that it has succeeded in promoting collective farming in many villages. Plots are collectively owned, loans are advanced from collective funds, grain is stored in a collective granery........ What their (CPML) sources do not agree upon is the suggestion that they have been sharpening caste conflicts by mobilising people from the backward caste against the upper caste landholders. On the contrary, they say their efforts have been to establish links with upper caste landholders and persuade them to concede higher wages or to surrender surplus land. It is only when the landholders try to resist or seek Police help, they said, that the conflicts start."[6]

References :

1. Rafiq Khan and Shivswarat Singh of the Gandhian Institute of Studies, Varanasi : 'Atrocities on Harijans in Bishrampur' (1978).
2. Nageshwar Prasad : "Rural Violence in India" (1985).
3. The Times of India, a national daily, Dt. 2nd May, 1986.
4. The Indian Express, a national daily, Dt. 8th December, 1986.
5. Nageshwar Prasad : "Rural Violence in India" (1985).
6. Uttam Sengupta in the Telegraph, a national daily published from Calcutta, Dt. 25th October, 1986.

CHAPTER 11

VIOLENCE AGAINST THE TRIBALS IN BIHAR

Singbhum district of Bihar forms part of the Southern Chotanagpur district and contains 15 hilly upland tracks. The area is extremely rich in forest and mineral resources. It is one of the largest sources of iron ore deposit in India. The main tribes of Adivasis who inhabit are : Ho and Munda. The forest is so important to the Advasis that they treat the forest as an object of worship and trees like Sal and Mahua to be sacred. They offer prayers to Singh Bonga (Sun God) and Baru Bonga (Mountain and Forest God) in a sacred grove of Saal Trees which they call as Sarna. The nationalisation of forests was a big blow to the Adivasis as they lost all their rights on the forest and its produce.

The tribal people of Kolhan area of Singbhum were independent till the early 19th Century. The British rule came to the area in 1821 and the Kolhans were subjugated for the first time. The British imposed a revenue system and appointed non-tribals as tax collectors. Within ten years, the Kolhans rose in rebellion agaisnt this exploitation. The movement spread over a large area and the British army moved in. Hundreds of tribal inhabitants of the Kolhans were gunned down before the Kolhan rebellion was finally crushed. Mr. P.C. Chowdhury records in the district gazetteer. "Kol revolt was indeed a national movement of the aboriginal. It had more right to be regarded as the first freedom struggle fought in India by the half civilized jungle folks than the movement of 1857. It was a widespread revolt of different sections of aboriginal people in Singhbum, Chota Nagpur and adjoining territories as a protest agaisnt inequalities, inefficiency and mal-administration by the British."

The gullibility, simplicity and illiteracy of the tribals have been exploited by the outsiders who got them to sign almost on blank sheets of paper and had taken over possession of their land for illegal mining. These outsiders have their contractors and agents to recruit tribal labour and send them out to several places as mine labourers.

A sociologist of the Punjab agricultural University has estimated that there are over one million migrant agricultural labourers in Punjab coming from the other States; the bulk of it, however, ranging upto 66% hail from Bihar tribal communities.[1] In spite of the industrialisation in Bihar, so many tribals migrate to other areas for jobs. Two reasons militate against the employment prospects of the tribals in industry:

1. Adequate technical education facilities do not exist for imparting necessary technical skill to the tribals;
2. the medium of instruction in primary schools is Hindi which is not their mother tongue. Since they cannot follow the Hindi language, there is a high rate of drop out. In chota Nagpur, although the tribals comprise almost 40% and in some parts even 60% of the total population, none of the major industries has a labour force of tribals which is more than 5%.[1]

Because of the severe hardships that the tribals had to undergo consequent on the acquisition of their land for establishment of large scale industries owing to availability of raw material closeby, the tribals have come to regard these natural resources more as a curse than a bounty of nature. Although compensation is paid for the land acquired, the tribals feel frustrated owing to denial of timely assistance. Certain projects have been providing employment to at least one member from each of the displaced families but this does not go far enough. Since most of the tribals are illiterate and lack technical skill and adaptability they end up as manual labourers.

The Jharkhand movement which seeks a separate state for the tribal districts has conferred a degree of prestige to the tribal identity. Though only seven out of the 31 districts of Bihar are included in the Jharkhand concept, it includes some other districts outside the State of Bihar. The seven districts of Bihar constitute a half of the geographical area of the State. 25% of the total population of Bihar reside in the area. Nearly a half of the total Scheduled Castes and Scheduled Tribe population of the State reside in this region. Chota Nagpur and Santhal Pargana together account for only a 40th part of the geographical area of the coutnry but more than ¼th of the total mining activities of the country take place in this small region. Nearly a fifth of India's total public sector investments in the industrial activities is located in this region[2]. Among the urban population, the Jharkhandis are slum dwellers. In industrial employment, the unskilled workers are Jharkhandis, the well-paid workers are outsiders. The contractors are outsiders. The labourers are recruited locally. Government policies have given rise to tribal resistance which has assumed the form of Jharkhand Mukti Morcha.

There have been reports of Police high-handedness against the tribals involving the death of some of them, which the police have not explained satisfactorily. One such case is the death of Ganga Ram Kalundia of Singbhum district who was killed on 4th April, 1982, allegedly by the police.

On 8th September, 1980 the Bihar Military Police opened fire at Gua in Singhbhum on an assembly of the Tribals organized by the Jharkhand Mukti Morcha, killing II and wounding 14 persons. Some of the injured Adivasis were taken to the hospital half a kilometre away. "But as soon as the first batch of Adivasis were brought to the hospital, they were surrounded and assulted and then shot dead. According to the official version, 9 rounds were fired killing 9 Adivasis within the Hospital compond."[3]

On lst Jun,1983 one gazetted police officer is alleged to have tied four Advasis to a jeep and driven the vehicle through the market place in Gua. After the drive, the Adivasis were taken out and beaten in which one of them died. Nothing was done to the Police Officer though he was briefly suspended from service. A six member Parliamentary Committee working for the welfare of the Scheduled Castes and Scheduled tribes confirmed the allegation of Police high-handedness. One of the tribal leaders alleged in the Bihar Assembly on 20th June, 1983 that the Police action in the tribal areas made nonsense of the Government's claim that it is committed to the welfare of the weaker sections.[4]

In the Sahibganj area of Bihar, the Adivasis were trying to assert their right to fish in a tank which was being denied to them by a money-lender, who had considerable influence locally with the officials concerned. Fifteen Adivasis were killed in Police firing which included one ex-MP who was at the time of the firing negotiating with one of the responsible officials. The circumstances of his death was one of the several mysteries that shroud this sordid affair. The Inquiry that followed justified the Police firing in its report.

It is alleged by the tribals that in the Kolhan area in Singbhum district there have been as many as 17 firings between August, 1982 and August, 1983, none of which was ever inquired into.

In incidents in which persons from the weaker sections are killed while trying to secure their rights, how much is too much and how long is too long? Apparently, endless waiting seems to be one of the primary occupations of these poor people.

To the non-tribals, however, the tribal land is a veritable eldorado. Land is available for grabbing, labour is for the asking and the simple tribal women can be seduced or molested. When certain villages were raided in the Santhal Pargana by the police in 1979, it was alleged that the men were beaten up and the women raped. As a sequel to this, the women are reported to have formed an organization called "WAR" (Women Against Rape). The raid against them was reportedly organized because of the resistance offered by the tribals to the land grab by some of the upper caste landholders.

Though the Bonded labour system was formally abolished in 1975, the labour released from the bondage have been recruited by contractors to work in brick kilns in Muzaffarpur, Samastipur and other places outside, on terms more dehumanising than those under the Bonded Labour system. The tribal girls who are recruited as labour get paid hardly Rs. 15/- a week. They are made to work for 12 to 14 hours a day and are sometimes exploited sexually. None of these suspected outrages can be fully authenticated in the absence of attendance register, employment cards (which are never maintained) and Labour Inspectors with commitment to enforce the Labour Laws.

The Koel-Karo Project in Ranchi in Bihar has affected nearly 6,739 tribal landowners and several thousand landless. The affected people had filed a writ in the Supreme Court to get rehabilitation and relief before they were dispossessed and evicted from the land. The Supreme Court appointed an Advocate to submit a report after an on the spot study of the problem. The Advocate, Jose Verghese reported to the Supreme Court in April, 1986. According to the report, the Government was acquiring land from other tribals who had meagre possessions of land to rehabilitate the dispossessed ones! The Advocate's finding was supported by documents to show that in the same area in which the tribal land was being acquired to rehabilitate the displaced tribals, there were also six non-tribal landowners owning a total of 7,740.33 acres. Two of these landowners have each 2439.69 acres and 2409.93 acres of land. Two others have 1337.8 and 1240.1 acres.[5] All these were left untouched. This gives an idea of not only how the land Ceiling Act has been flouted but even later how these were left untouched, when marginal holdings of poor tribals were acquired. By not acquiring the land from non-tribals, but only from the poorer tribals for rehabilitating the affected tribals, the authorities opened themselves to the charge that they are discriminating against the tribals. The tribals affected by the Koel-Karo Project had been extremely agitated.

The Tribal Welfare Commissioner submitted a report to the Government in 1982 stating that the tribals felt aggrieved on account of the inadequate monetary compensation paid to them for the land acquired from them in connection with various projects.

The National Labour Institute had undertaken a study in February, 1984 of the wages and working conditions of the mine workers in Singbhum district. The report has pointed out large-scale illegal mining in areas where the tribals are the legitimate owners of the land. They are denied adequate compensation. Minimum wages are never paid to the workers. Several mines do not keep records regarding the number of workers, wage payment, etc. The study has pointed out several serious infringements of the different provisions of the Labour Laws and ruthless exploitation of the ignorant and illiterate Adviasis by the contractors.

At the instance of the Supreme Court, Advocate. Jose Verghese visited Singhbhum district of Bihar earlier in Feburary, 1984 to ascertain the status of the cases pending against tribals in the district. Hundreds of cases were pending for years for filing of charge sheets by the police under the Forest Act, Excise Act, Indian Penal Code and others. In all these cases the accused tribals were either in jail or on bail. Mr. Verghese in the course of his report[6] to the Supreme Court had observed: "It was shocking to note that in absolute denial of justice to the poor Adivasis in Singbhum and in gross violation of the fundamental rights, there were more than 3,790 cases against the Adivasis which were pending for several years without any charge sheet in the various courts. In some of these cases, the accused were also in jail for more than three to four years. An examination of the list of 1623 Forest cases instituted against the Adivasis during the period from 1978 to 1983 shows that there are many instances where on the same day a person who was accused in one particular case was alleged to have been accused in as many as 8 different cases in different locations."

The Supreme Court, disposing of the writ petition filed in 1983 by Mathew Areeparampil and others against the illegal and indiscriminate detention of Advivasis by the State of Bihar observed in its order dated 20th September, 1984: "The facts as gleaned from the reports and documents reveal a most shocking state of affairs in the region in question. It seems that a very large number of people have been languishing in jails without trial for petty offences." When repeated instances of such callousness on the part of the authorities towards the tribals occur, the tribals and their leaders understandably feel agitated and aggrieved that they are not being given a fair deal. These experiences in no small measure contribute to their alienation from the mainstream of national life.

N.E. Horo, one of the important tribal leaders had once observed: "In tackling the tribal question, the Government of India is ultimately concerned with the assimilation and integration of the tribals in the mainstream of Indian society the majority dominant Hindu society....... If assimilation in Hindu society is a noble process, how is that the Harijans are struggling against social subjugation?...... for the Indian tribals the question is whether to be in bondage or to be free, whether to be submerged or to retain their identity. Tribals are Indian and they will remain Indian. They should find their place of honour as Indian tribals."

The demand for a separate Jharkhand State or Union Territory status for areas comprising Chota Nagpur plateau and the Santhal Pargana districts was raised by the Jharkhand Mukti Morcha on the Jharkhand Mukti Diwas celebrated by 70,000 tribal men, women and children in Dumka and Dhanbad in February, 1986. The zeal and fervour of the tribals on the occasion was reportedly unprecedented. As Suraj Mandal who is a tribal M.L.A. put it: "every young man here is now ready to become Sidho and Kano, the legendary Santhal brothers, who raised the banner of revolt against the British and the Mahjans 130 years ago." The tribals would be able to prove on the basis of facts on the ground that they have not had a very fair deal under the existing dispensation. This can be one of the sources of continuing violence as it has been in the past, if things are allowed to drift.

References :

1. Scenario of the 7% Volume 2 by : Cinemart Foundation, C-6/9 Safdarjung Development Area, New Delhi.
2. Nirmal Sengupta in the Economic and Political Weekly, Dt. 5th April, 1980.
3. A.K. Roy, M.P., in the Economic and Political Weekly, Dt. 21st February, 1981.
4. The Times of India, a national daily, Dt. 21st June, 1983.
5. Report of Advocate Jose Verghese, Dt. April, 1985.
6. Report of Advocate Jose Verghese, Dt. February, 1984 on the Criminal cases pending against the Tribals.

CHAPTER 12

VIOLENCE IN UTTAR PRADESH

Fake encounters with dacoits:

In village Dehuli of Mainpuri district in Uttar Pradesh in October, 1981 violence by the dacoits reached one of its highest peaks in what has come to be referred to as the 'Dehuli Carnage' in which more than 20 persons were killed by dacoits. The then Chief Minister of Uttar Pradesh responded to this carnage with a declaration that he would finish the dacoit menace in a month's time. This was a signal for the police to step up their activities. The result was a series of 'encounters'. Prof. Juyal of the Gandhian Institute of Studies observes in his study[1]: "Though the State Government has been dishing out conflicting figures about the encounter deaths, according to one set of figures, there were 2860 encounters until November, 1980 in which 1,162 persons were killed. The figures for four years until the end of 1981 stood at 7,879(?) killed in encounters. 228 persons were killed just inside one month from November 24th to December 24th, 1981. The encounters were being 'targetted' from above."

There were public protests against the stage managed encounters. Political parties staged demonstrations and agitations against the so called encounters. Detailed memoranda with names of victims allegedly killed in encounters were submitted to the State Government demanding inquiry into the incidents. Even some ruling party legislators expressed their doubts about the encounters. The Government, however, refused to give in on the ground that the inquires would only demoralise the police, who, the Government felt, was doing their job. Professor

Juyal has quoted the findings of the Uttar Pradesh and Madhya Pradesh Sarvodaya Mandals who had constituted a fact-finding team of important office bearers to study the facts and circumstances of police encounters in Jhansi district. Their conclusions were: "After extensive tour through Jhansi district where the police claims to have killed five bad characters as a result of four successful encounters recently, the team found that none of these were 'encounters' and all the five persons were picked up and killed by the police in a planned manner and later shown as killed in 'encounters'[2].

Professor B.N. Juyal had come to the conclusion that many of the 'encounters' were nothing but cold-blooded murders and as many as 80% of the victims belonged to the Scheduled Castes. At worst many of them may have been petty criminals if at all, or they might have had the temerity to stand up on behalf of the weaker sections against the oppression of the locally influential persons, official or non-official. In many cases, the police records, in so far as they reflect any criminal activities of the victims, were woefully unconvincing.

By themselves some of these cases showed police high-handedness. But what is more appalling and a matter of serious concern is that, in some of these cases the Police Officers at the Police Station level had acted at the instance of vested interests or feudal lords owing to petty personal or caste considerations. Such incidents are indicators not only of the continuance of the exploitative caste and class conflicts which characterise the rural scene in some districts of Uttar Pradesh but subversion of the police. In spite of the police 'encounters' and the liquidation of hundreds of so-called dacoits, the incidence of dacoities in some of these districts had not decreased. In fact the very police stations which were reporting higher numbers of encounter killings, were also having higher incidence of dacoities. This was possibly because the real dacoits were not killed in the 'encounters' but some innocents, and there was a backlash arising from the resentment of the innocents.

Dacoity in these areas has come to be used as a smoke screen for caste and occasionally class repression, and has ceased to be a criminal act by anti-social elements. It is becoming one of the substreams of the socio-political process. Its relevance and utility in the political context in some of the states is demonstrated repeatedly at the time of elections. The presence of some of the extremely active and ruthless dacoit gangs in some of the states has an additional dimension which normally does not come to notice with the same sharpness as the manifest activities of the gangs themselves. These outlaws have the benefit of back up in terms of safe havens, suppliers of weapons and sharers of booty which are all done by persons some of whom are politicians, who also provide indemnity to dacoits from being caught. In return the dacoits provide politicians their muscle and money power at the time of elections. These dacoits command a vote bank in villages because of the terror they have struck in the minds of the people of the area. This fear is exploited during elections to swing the votes to suit their needs. It is impossible to beat this system because no witness is willing to stake his life and property by coming forward to tender oral evidence against such influential persons.

That some of the dacoits in Uttar Pradesh enjoy political protection is a very well known fact. In the recent past there was the case of the dacoit Gaya Kurmi who had committed several docoities and other crimes in Banda district. When he finally surrendered and was lodged in jail pending trial, the local MLA approached the Government with an application recommending that the undertrial dacoit be accorded a level of treatment, higher than the one he was entitled to. This was agreed to by the Government. Subsequently, it was reversed because of the strong intervention by the district authorities at the decision making level.

One of the compelling reasons which drives even ordinary law abiding citizens to take law into their own hands is the loss of faith in the ability of the criminal justice system to deliver speedy and certain justice. There are hundreds of examples which reinforce the belief that a man who feels intensely aggrieved can settle scores only by taking law into his own hands instead of waiting for the judicial process to grind slowly with doubtful result at the end of it. This aspect of the working of the criminal justice system is one of the important factors contributing to violence in its cruelest form in the countryside. Amidst the clamour about the atrocities on the weaker sections in the rural areas, one tends to lose sight of the basic conditions which create and contribute towards these atrocities. We tend to take notice only when the problems erupt into inconvenient and non-acceptable forms of physical violence. We, however, are not willing to go deeper into the cause of violence in an effort to sort matters out on the basis of social justice and fairplay. As long as the dispossessed, disadvantaged and the exploited are willing to suffer in silence without raising a word of protest, we feel complacent that these areas need not to be disturbed, lest we should raise the hornet's nest. As long as this attitude permeates the political and administrative systems, we will never be able to plug the sources of violence which lurk in the very iniquity of the systems. This calls for political perspicacity and administrative norms which should be for ever animated by a social conscience directed towards social justice.

The Yamuna-Chambal lower basin districts lying south of Agra-Allahabad axis in Uttar Pradesh have been the scene of unmitigated violence by dacoits against the defenceless villagers during the last several years and more so during the early eighies. This type of violence is not new to the area. At no stage can it be said to have been completely free from the depredations of the dacoits and the violence that had gone with it. Efforts made from time to time to deal with the problem had only resulted in ceremonial "surrenders" of some of the leading dacoits who were thereafer subjected to favourable dispensation and prosecuted. The wisdom of tackling the dacoit problem by such populist procedures which have invariably been conceived and executed at the highest level of the State Government have always been doubted by the people but only once publicly called into question. This was when Shri K.F. Rustamji was the Inspector General of Police of Madhya Pradesh. He disapproved of the measures taken by a person of the stature of Vinoba Bhava in the late fifties to get some of the dacoits operating in the Chambal ravines to surrender to the authorities. In retrospect one marvels at the foresight and comprehension of Shri K.F. Rustamji who could anticipate nearly thirty years ago, the futility of such surrenders and the gross miscarriage of justice that accompanies the trials of some of the surrendered dacoits. The problem of dacoits continues to be with us in spite of these pompous and highly publicised "surrenders". The extra dimension that this problem has acquired over the years is the political clout that the surrendering dacoits have come to enjoy and which is derived from the patronage that they receive from the politicians, who in turn use the dacoits for terrorising the voters and intimidating their political opponents at the time of elections.

The Madhya Pradesh Police conducted a study of their experience in dealing with the surrendered dacoits. Some of their conclusions are: The ceremonial surrenders that have become a feature of the menace of dacoities in some of States were usually preceded by verbal assurances to the surrendering dacoits that by and large a lenient view would be taken about the sentences to be awarded to them and that they would be kept in special jails and given facilities for meeting their relatives. They were promised that their dependents would be provided with employment. The witnesses were reluctant to give evidence because of the special consideration extended to the surrendered dacoits by the administration and the police. The surrendred dacoits were given comforts such as fans and cooking arrangements in the jail. Since the prosecution had to be launched within a stipulated time and the number of cases to be investigated was large, the police invariably had a difficult time. The advantages from this naturally accrued to the dacoits. The situation was made worse by the attitude of the surrendered dacoits who, through their relations and friends terrorised the witnesses. The study came to the conclusion that the system of ceremonial surrender of dacoits was responsible for the growth of new gangs. Public impression was that persons who could amass wealth by committing dacoities could also get away with their crimes by conveniently surrendering at a later stage and availing of the various rehabilitation schemes extended by the Government to the surrendered dacoits. Thus the dacoits had nothing to lose in this arrangement.

In dealing with the surrendered dacoits, criminal justice system has been applied in a grossly selective manner. They had killed in cold blood defenceless people in dozens and the degree of notoriety achieved by them was measured in terms of the amount of reward announced by the Government to get the dacoit dead or alive. Yet, the treatment accorded to them and the manner in which their prosecution was handled were in such sharp and invidious contrast to the vexatious manner in which an ordinary petty criminal is put through the processes of law. A case in point is of Phoolan, the woman dacoit, who continues to enjoy state-organised preferential treatment in Gwalior Jail. She had not been handed over even after about four years to the Uttar Pradesh Police where she is required in 74 cases of gruesome murder and dacoities. The Madhya Pradesh Police was concerned with her only in connection with some petty Arms Act violations. When the scales of justice are held so very unevenly, with the full knowledge and concurrence of the Government, one cannot expect an ordinary citizen to have respect for justice and equity. The cases of some of the surrendered dacoits prove that mass murders and ruthless dacoities committed in cold-blood and on multiple occasions cease to be crimes, as we understand them normally. what gets the raw end of justice is petty crime indulged in by the indigent and the deprived. With such an approach to the dispensation of justice, how can one expect violence to disappear from society? Such invidious treatment is, a standing invitation to more and greater violence.

References:

1. Professor Juyal of the Gandhian Institute of Studies, Varanasi : "Encounter killings of dacoits the phase of repression in a peasant society" (1985).
2. IBID

CHAPTER 13

CASTE CONFLICTS IN UTTAR PRADESH

A perusal of some of the daily papers published from any of the crime prone districts in Uttar Pradesh gives a very good insight into the chronic causes that generate violence in some of these districts. It gives an idea of the fate of the land reforms and the manner in which it is thwarted by moneyed interests in collusion with village officials. Some of these reports give an idea of the caste conflicts that persist in society even after four decades of Independence. Most of the violence is a product of the social change that is being sought to be imposed from above, since the change would not evolve by itself fast enough from below, especially in the absence of any serious effort by voluntary organizations specially committed to act as agents of change.

In an incident reported from Pilibhit district towards the end of 1985, one Harijan was killed and 14 others injured, 7 of them seriously, when the school authorities objected to the funeral procession of a nine-years-old Harijan girl being taken by the side of the junior school. When the Harijans insisted on taking that route, they were fired upon.

On 6th December, 1985, 4 Harijans were shot down and six others including three women were injured, 5 of them seriously in disrict Ballia. The multiple murder was due to dispute over land. The immediate provocation was provided by the Harijans plucking leaves from a bamboo cluster located in the disputed area.

Ironically enough the welfare measures intended for the uplift and betterment of weaker sections have been the direct causes of much manifest violence against these sections. The social and economic change that is being sought to be brought about in their economic position and living conditions has been accompanied by horrendous birth pangs. The Harijans have occasionally, under some of their intrepid leaders, stood up and fought. They too have produced their dacoit leaders, for example the ex-serviceman who came to be known as 'Fouzy', who led his own gang of dacoits in Banda district as a reaction against the continued repression to which the Harijans had been subjected.

The depredations of dacoits in Uttar Pradesh are largely based on caste considerations. A gang which was operating in Banda during 1985 and early 1986 was a gang led by a Kurmi caste leader. This gang specialises in kidnapping for ransom. Their victims were almost exclusively from the Brahmin caste. This was intended as a reprisal against the past domination and oppression of the Kurmis by the Brahmins. As a result the entire village inhabited by Kumis extend help to the Kurmi gang in many ways and this inevitably rendered the job of the police to run to ground the gang extremely difficult. In the meantime, tension continued and with it a general sense of insecurity in the entire area.

In Jalaon district of Uttar Pradesh there has been so much violence traditionally that it is customary to correlate the quantity of grains produced at the end of the harvest by the number of murders that are committed. The women belonging to a certain community are so revengeful that if their husbands are killed they would not consider themselves as widows till the death of their husbands is avenged either through their sons or their brothers. What is important is that indulging in violence and settling scores with rivals even through murders do not result in stigma and the society accepts the offenders. In fact, it is the hall-mark of heroism for a young man to avenge the death of his father or brother. In the process, he fulfils the expectations that people have of him. This sociological aspect is another important factor contributing to violence. It is not unusual for children to be named after the dacoits nor is it uncommon for a man to sell his wife in order to purchase a gun for avenging the murder of one of his relations. The terrain, full of ravines facilitates the hide-out of the violent criminals who become fugitives from law.

There is a community of Dadi Thakur spread over about 84 villages of Kanpur and Jalaon districts. They are noted for the facility with which they resort to violence even at the slightest provocation. Some of the notorious dacoits who had indulged in mass murders belonged to this region. It was actually to avenge the rape committed on Phoolan, the woman dacoit, by some of the Thakurs that Phoolan is alleged to have committed the murder of 21 Thakurs in a single incident in village Bahamai of Kanpur district. Many cases of Kidnapping for ransom take place in Jalaon district, as the people in this area are flush with liquid cash. Disputes over land are endemic. The disputes culminate inevitably in violence. The deposition by witnesses in courts in favour of or against those indulging in violence invites its own retribution. In Unnao district a witness who had signed a seizure memo at the instance of the police was murdered. Many of the criminals who indulge in violence on one ground or the other and are fugitives from law get the support and protection of their own caste people as also some of the local politicians, a feature which is not peculiar to this area anyway.

In the incident of 22nd July, 1985 in Singhpur in Kanpur district, 6 persons were shot dead by five persons whose names were known. One of the persons who was an accused in this case was a police Constable in the district of Lucknow and he had used his licenced fire arm for committing the offence. Though there was a long standing rivalry between the two groups, the immediate provocation was the election for the post of Gram Pradhan in which a Harijan by name Ram Kishan, who was one of the deceased had contested against a Thakur who was the rival group leader. It is yet one more incident of violent retaliation by the upper caste power lobbies against the feeble challenges of Harijans, aspiring for a say in local political afairs.

The following incident is so very shocking that it deserves mention even though it took place in a district situated in Madhya Pradesh bordering Jhansi district of Uttar Pradesh. In village Naugaon near Bina in the Sagar district of Madhya Pradesh, an Upasarpanch who was a Harijan had to pay with his life for having had the temerity to illuminate his house with electric lights on the occasion of the marriage of his daughter. The display of electric lamps at the marriage Pandal outraged a section of the people of the village. The matter figured in the proceedings of the Madhya Pradesh State Assembly on March 18, 1986. The Minister of State for Home, making a statement in the Assembly observed that a person "apparently enraged that a Harijan had used electric tubelights, entered the Pandal and smashed some tubelights. Later the body of the Upsarpanch was found in a nearby field."[1]

The riots that took place in Agra on 3rd May, 1978 between the Harijans (Jatavs) and the upper castes over the problems arising out of the Ambedkar Jayanti celebrations of 14th April, 1978 was of a very serious nature. In the fight that ensued between the police and the Jatavs, there was police firing and large scale arson. Buses in different parts of the city were burnt, telephone wires were cut, fish plates were removed from railway tracks, and attempts to set fire to a petrol pump in Agra were reported, all allegedly done by the Jatav mobs.

The Army was called in aid of the civil power. The number of Jatavs dead was reportedly nine including two women, while many more persons including those of the police force were seriously injured. This incident had one special feature which needs to be taken note of. Jatav and other Harijan leaders from far off places including the South are reported to have converged on Agra with food, money and medical help. Owen M. Lynch writing in Economic and Political Weekly observed[2] : "Over and over again the Jatav themselves said to me that violence had united them despite their varying political persuasion. All, even the conservative Jatav leaders, said that Ambedkar's diagnosis of and remedy for the caste situation had been right; the only way was to take the offensive, to fight and fight back. While inspecting the scenes of the riots with them, Jatavs expressed pride in their ability to fight back and meet violence with violence."

In certain districts in Uttar Pradesh such as Unnao and Azamgarh, Dhobis who are Scheduled Caste have gone to the Middle East and are earning well, remit this money to their families in the villages. The new found affluence among the Dhobis has aroused the jealousy of the upper castes and there have been conflicts on that account. The Indian Embassies abroad have reportedly been writing to the District Magistrates to give protection to the relations of the migrants staying behind in the villages.

In the context of the social change in the rural area, the Government of Uttar Pradesh have in their anxiety to protect the weaker sections, taken special steps to ensure that complaints emanating from the Scheduled Castes should be carefully attended. There are cases of the upper castes exploiting this particular directive to settle dispute between themselves by using a Scheduled Caste individual or group as a tool in their fight. They use a Scheduled Caste individual to complain against the rival group exploiting thereby the special machinery set up to attend to the Scheduled Caste complaints. The rival party gets harassed even though in the process what is sought to be settled is a non-existent dispute between the rival party and the Harijans.

Even the administration appears to have veered round to the belief that by and large only administrators belonging to the same caste can be trusted to look after the interests of the people belonging to their respective castes. This in turn is based on the feeling that administrators are incapable of transcending caste considerations in administrative matters which concern people belonging to other castes. Once a pernicious belief of this type comes to be accepted and acted upon, we are not far from the interests of the State being taken over by the caste leaders with all the conflict and violence that it will generate. Whether the road to this situation was paved with a series of failures at the various levels of dispensation of justice to those who supplicated for it, or whether it was motivated by the anxiety of the Government to provide double insurance, it is a sad reflection on the credibility of the official machinery and its unreliability and partisanship. It is in this context that the creation of special cells at the district and police station levels to watch the interest of the weaker sections have to be viewed. Such arrangements only run counter to the climate that the Government seeks to create; In fact it undermines the integrity and self-confidence of the administration.

References

1. The Hindu, a national daily, Dt. 20th March. 1986.
2. Owen M. Lynch : "Rioting as rational action: An interpretation of the April. 1981 riots in Agra" in the Economic and Political Weekly Dt. 28th November, 1981.

CHAPTER 14

BONDED LABOUR

When there is an act on the statute book the provisions of which are not enforced, it can have two effects : It can be misused by several functionaries of the Government in extracting illegal gratification for the violation of the relevant provisions by the offending parties concerned; and over a period of time, non-compliance with the law if allowed to go unchallenged breeds in the people a disrespect for law which in turn can lead to violence in one form on another.

This aspect of the consequences of non-enforcement of existing social legislation is nowhere better illustrated than in relation to the problems of Bonded Labour. The practice is evidently an infringement of human dignity and a violation of human rights. It packs into the system very much of potent and manifest violence and it continues to be practised in all its degrading aspects even now as in the past. The number of such cases may have become marginally smaller.

"There is no use having social welfare laws on the statute book if they are not going to be implemented. One must not be content with the law in books but we must have law in action." These are the observations of the Supreme Court in a judgement delivered on December 16, 1983 in a case related to the Bonded Labour working in stone quarries in Faridabad district of Haryana.

In another case reported in late 1985, the District Judge of Tehri Garhwal himself visited a place following the direction by the Supreme Court on a writ petition filed by a local Advocate on behalf of the Bonded Labourers. The Judge found to his utter shock that 100 bonded labourers were being kept in a cage made of tin along with cooking fuel, rice and wheat. The cage was of 50' by 60' in dimension and part of it was covered by gunny bags. Seven labourers were lying ill without any medical attention. The labourers told the District Judge that they were paid Rs. 2/- or Rs. 3/- per wek and some of them were paid a wage of fifty paise for vegetables three times a week. The minimum wages prescribed is Rs. 16.65 per day. These laourers who had been recruited from Bihar and Orissa had been paid a loan of Rs. 600/- initially. Much of what they could receive was adjusted against the original debt which never gets liquidated in full. The Supreme Court took cognizance of the report and directed the State to take action against the parties who were violating the labour laws and rules. The District Judge observed : "I have no hesitation in saying that the Labour Inspector was guilty of having stated before me the wrong information, concealing the truth and not taking any interest in the welfare of the labourers probably to help and promote the management for reasons best known to him."

The Bonded Labour Abolition Act envisaged setting up of vigilance committees as the main instrument for enforcing the Act. Dr. R.K. Tiwari of the Indian Institute of Public Administration who conducted a study of the implementation of the Act in six districts in the country has observed[1] : "In Tehri Garhwal district of Uttar Pradesh, the Tehri subdivision vigilance committee did not function at all. It was defective in composition to such an extent that at least one of the members had 18 bonded labourers serving under him. These Committees mainly concentrated on devising ways and means of getting allowances, while matters related to Bonded Labourers were hardly discussed." Dr. Tiwari had observed that in all the six districts surveyed by him, more than 90% of the bonded labour were from the Scheduled Castes and Scheduled Tribes living with their employers. In many cases the head of the family or the entire family served as bonded labourers.

Mr. Yogendra Makwana, who was the Union Minister of State for Agriculture in 1984 is reported to have admitted :

"Efforts for the liberation of bonded labourers have remained incomplete in all states due to the half hearted approach adopted by them." Attributing the bureaucracy's lack of involvement in the programmes to the absence of political and administrative will in the State, Makwana also gave some startling instances where supposedly rehabilitated bonded labourers were still under bondage serving their masters, while others due to inadequate subsistance had taken to begging.[2]

The number of bonded labour in the country as estimated by the Gandhi Peace Foundation stood at 2.62 million. According to H. Pais, Dean of the National Labour Institute, this estimate is the most authentic of all. According to the Ministry of Labour, which operates a scheme for rehabilitation of bonded labour, the total number of bonded labour identified so far is 0.21 million. Out of this, 0.16 million have been rehabilitated. Thus, the total number of bonded labour identified by the Ministry of Labour is less than 10% of the number estimated by Gandhi Peace Foundation. H. Pais has obsered in his paper on "Unorganised Labour" : "What is surprising is that the process of identification by the states has fallen into disuse and the number being identified every year is becoming smaller and smaller, giving rise to the impression that we are reaching the end of the problem...... Apparently governments have lost interest in this vital area, despite repeated expression of concern for the unorganised labour".

According to a report prepared by the Planning Commission in 1986 on the subject of rehabilitation of the labour released from the bondage : "Practically in all States no steps had been taken by the concerned authorities to assess the background and choice of the beneficiaries in the matter of allotment of rehabilitation schemes. This exposed most of the labour to the danger of reverting back to bondage."[3]

The Supreme Court had expressed pain and anguish over the delay on the part of the Commissioner South

Chotanagpur division, Ranchi, Bihar in furnishing information regarding the fate of about 617 bonded children. The children all below 14 years, working as bonded labour were earlier rescued under the Court's orders from the clutches of the carpet weaving factory owners in Mirzapur district of Uttar Pradesh. The Supreme Court observed: "We do not know though several months have passed as to the fate of the identified children and whether any steps have been taken for their rehabilitation. It is difficult to understand why the Commissioner has not made any report. The authorities should be sensitive to the problem of children forced to work in the carpet industry even though they are of tender age and their employment in such industry is prohibited under the Employment of Children Act."[4]

The foregoing instances of cruelly exploitative practices, be it in Bihar or in Uttar Pradesh, should leave us in no doubt about the fact that parts of the States of Bihar and Uttar Pradesh are plagued by near endemic violence open or disguised. Why is it then that we have not yet made progress in ascertaining the root causes of the evil and to take effective action to eradicate it? An inquiry of this nature will enable us to identify the problems and come up with solutions which will have relevance to the socio-economic conditions or the absence of institutional arrangements or the administrative inadequacies or may be traceable to political mismanagement. Instead, we seem to be treating each individual case as an isolated incident to be handled and disposed of by the police and the Court each in its *ad hoc* and time-consuming ways. That the intervening periods between the trials are punctuated by more and more violence and oppression does not make any appreciable difference to our entire approach to the problem.

References

1. Dr. R.K. Tiwari of the Indian Institute of Public Administration "Implementation of the Bonded Labour Act in six districts of the country" (1985).

2. Teesta Setalwad in the Indian Express, Dt. 25th August, 1985.
3. The Statesman, a national daily, Dt. 11th November, 1986.
4. The Hindu, a national daily, Dt. 29th October, 1986.

CHAPTER 15

CASTE CONFLICTS IN MAHARASHTRA

The Rise of the Mahars :

According to Jayant Lele[1], the Maratha Kumbi cluster occupy a very dominant position in Maratha politics. This contributed to the hegemony that they exercised over the socio-economic set up of rural Maharashtra. They constitute the bulk of the landed gentry in the rural areas. Though immediately after the reign of the Peshwas, the Brahmins had a predominant position with regard to the land holdings, their grip gradually weakened because of several factors that intervened. The share of the Maratha Kumbi class cluster with regard to the land holdings increased over the years. They took over the land owned by Brahmins as the Brahmins converged to the urban centres on account of the compaign against them following Gandhiji's assassination by a Brahmin. Even earlier the Brahmins had become increasingly absentee landholders because of their pre-occupation with the services and professional callings such as law and medicine.

The Marathas have a distinct culture of their own. In the social set up in the rural areas, the Marathas occupy a pre-eminent position and the Scheduled Castes, largely composed of the Mahars, the Mangs and the Bhangis used to be spatially separated from the village location. Even so life revolved around a pattern of inter-dependence. There was however, no doubt that the Scheduled Castes were a community dependent on the Marathas. They were called upon to perform the menial tasks. The Mahars, as distinct from the Mangs and the Bhangis, also peformed important social functions as village officials and over a period of time they came to acquire a status derived from their official functions and responsibilities which was distinct from and much higher than that occupied by the other Scheduled Castes. This had bred in them a strong sense of self-importance which in later years manifested itself as rebelliousness against the system. This official background gave to the Mahars a status which has played a very useful role in the social change that is affecting them.

Social reformation had begun to take place in Maharashtra from the time of Jotirao Phule (1827-1890). Phule was a critic of the Brahmin-Maratha hegemony though he himself belonged to the Maratha community. Phule also tried to organize the peasants against money lenders and the landholders. One important characteristic of the anti-Brahmin movement in Maharashtra is that it did not come about either as a sequel to or a consequence of the oppression by the Brahmins of the other caste groups. In a sense, it was incidental to the ascendancy and assertion of the socio-economic dominance of the Marathas in the socio-political scenario. Phule had attempted to mobilise all the backward classes with a view to establishing a society based on the principles of the welfare of all. The anti-Brahmin movement was primarily limited to the elite among the Marathas. The lower classes among the lower castes were not active participants in the movement.

The history of the emancipation of the Mahar community among the Scheduled Castes in Maharashtra from the oppression of the dominant castes dates back to the twenties of the century. Jayshreé B. Gokhale has dealt with this very lucidly in her paper.[2] According to her, in Maharashtra 6% are Brahmins; the Maratha Kumbi class cluster account for 40%; and the Scheduled Castes, Scheduled Tribes and Bhuddhists constitute about 19%. Dr. B.R. Ambedkar who provided the leadership to the Mahar movement was as much a legend when he was alive as he is when he is dead. The history of the Mahars voicing their resentment against the upper caste domination dates back to their first major satyagraha which was launched in March, 1972 at Mahad in

Colaba district of the Konkan. This movement was designed to enforce equal accesss to the community water supply to the so-called untouchables. Another movement in the 1930s demanded the right of temple entry for Harijans. These movement were largely spearheaded by the Mahar community. The Mahad agitation of March, 1927 encouraged Ambedkar to launch another agitation at the same venue in December, 1927. The December conference was marked by the burning of the Manusmriti which sent shock waves through Hindu society, incensing the orthodox among them. This was considered an open challenge to the Hindu society. The symbolic gesture was intended to demonstrate to the Scheduled Castes, that the laws which kept them in bondage had no divine sanction, that they were entirely man-made, and as such could be destroyed by man. The same act was repeated by the Dalit Panthers fifty years later later in 1977 in Marathawada region, and which produced the same rage and resentment among the upper caste Hindus. These movements helped in heightening the Mahar consciousness resulting in concrete action. The Mahar Regiment of the Indian Army which gave a good account of itself in the Second World War, understandably gave the Mahars a pride of place and honour in the Indian nation.

The next important milestone in mobilising the Mahars under the leadership of Dr. Ambedkar was the conversion ceremony to Buddhism at Nagpur in 1956. According to an estimate, 55% of the Mahars had got converted to Buddhism. It was also generally concluded that it was only the Mahars, who became Buddhists, leaving out the other constituents of the Scheduled Caste spectrum. The rejection of Hindu deities and the increased assertiveness of the Mahar Buddhists for their rights, such as access to the village well had led to angry retaliation by some sections of the villagers and more recently, it had led to a chain reaction of riots in Marathwada in 1978. The Mahar Buddhists acquired a new sense of identity and self-affirmation by repudiating the Hindu-religion.

This newly acquired sense of superiority, while antagonizing the Hindus, had also to an extent antagonized the other elements among the Scheduled Castes such as the Mangs and the Chamars. Despite the claim of the Mahars that they were leading the movement for the entire spectrum of the Scheduled Castes, in actual practice it turned out to be a movement exclusively of the Mahars, and the purport of this exclusiveness has not been lost on the Mangs and the Chamars. Vithal Ambedkar, a leading Mang intellectual pointed out that if Dr. Ambedkar was really interested in the Dalits, he should have encouraged inter-marriage among the untouchables themselves, which Ambedkar did not propagate. Hence, the ideology of the Dalit movement has failed to arouse and enthuse all the elements among the Scheduled Castes. On the contrary, it has accentuated the difference between them.[3]

In Maharashtra the elite among the Scheduled Caste population are not drawn from a cross section of the different groups that constitute the Scheduled Castes. Amongst them, one group which has benefitted the most is the Mahars and even among the Mahars, the group which has had the best deal is the Mahar Buddhists.

According to Jayashree Gokhale there are 57 groups among the Scheduled Castes in Maharashtra. Of these, the Mahars, the Mangs and Chamars constitute 90% of the total Scheduled Caste population. In the field of education, these three groups secured 96.6% of the post-matric scholarships. Even among this group of three, the Mahars who constitute 35.11% of the Scheduled Castes had cornered 82.8% of the scholarships in 1967-1968. The Mang community which is 33% of the Scheduled Caste population received 3.8% of the scholarships in 1967-1968. The Chamars with 22% of the Scheduled Caste population obtained 9.9%. This comparative data is not available for the later years. This disparity has generated a degree of jealousy and animosity against the Mahars from the other scheduled caste groups.

References

1. Jayant Lele of the Queens University. Kingston. Canada : "Caste. Class and Hegemony dominance" (1984).
2. Jayashree B. Gokhale : "Evolution of Counter Ideology. Dalit Consciousness in Maharashtra" (1984). (University of Delaware. Newark U.S.A.)
3. IDIB.

CHAPTER 16

MARATHWADA AGITATION

In July 1977, the Dalit Panthers (a group of militant Scheduled Castes youth who seem to have taken the American Black Panthers as their semantic model) took a decision to secure for the Neo-Buddhists all the concessions as are enjoyed by the Scheduled Caste people, including those in the Central Government services. They also demanded re-naming the Marathwada University after Dr. Baba Saheb Ambedkar. Though a resolution was passed by the University Executive Council recommending that the University be named after Dr. Ambedkar, the Senate at its meeting on 30th October, 1977 did not consider the resolution as the mover was absent. The issue assumed importance again from May, 1978. The non-Dalit students body started agitating against the proposed change by the Dalits. On 27th July, 1978 a resolution renaming the Marathwada University after Dr. Baba Saheb Ambedkar was adopted unanimously both in the Legislative Assembly and Council. The news of this decision was broadcast over All India Radio the same evening. It has, however, not yet been given effect to so far.

As soon as the news about the change was announced, those sections of the student community who were against the change took the agitation to the streets and attacked the residences of the leaders of the Dalit Panthers. A large number of Dalits were affected. Although the Dalit students in urban areas took the initiative, in the rural areas the agitation was spearheaded by non-Dalit communities. Some of the important features of the agitation were :

1) The state Administration was caught in a sudden and widespread agitation, which made it difficult to cope with it in the initial stages;

2) Some Government functionaries in villages joined hands in committing atrocities on Scheduled Castes and Neo-Buddhists;
3) Social workers and voluntary agencies were conspicuous by their absence in bringing about normality and restoring confidence among the victims.

One of the major factors responsible for heightening the tension between the caste Hindus and Dalits was that a large number of caste Hindus in the rural areas whose economic conditions were comparable to those of many of the Scheduled Castes, were resentful of the concessions by way of grant of land, job reservations and admission to professional institutions which were extended to the Scheduled Castes.

Government property, particularly the State Transport and the Railways were the main targets of attack during the agitation. During the agitation, a total of 227 villages were affected of which the Scheduled Castes in 169 villages were attacked. The police had to resort to large-scale lathi-charge, use of teargas and firing. The situation was brought under complete control by August 7, 1978.

The fate of the criminal cases arising out of the agitation registered by the police makes a very depressing reading. According to information received from a very authentic source, out of 153 cases of atrocities against the Harijans and the Neo-Buddhists registered during the Marathwada University agitation in six districts in 1978, 86 cases were sent up for trial. Of these 85 were still pending trial in March, 1986 and one was withdrawn. 58 cases were still under investigation. With such tardy follow up on cases of atrocities, one wonders whether the half-hearted criminal prosecution that is being resorted to by the police has any relevance to higher social objectives. This situation carries its own indictment of the inadequacies and ineffectiveness of the Criminal Justice System, which is in urgent need of repair, rejuvenation and even total transformation to attune it to the wide and fast changing socio-economic parameters in the country.

The Marathwada agitation of 1978 recorded a bench mark in the history of inter-caste conflicts in Maharashtra. That the caste Hindus were extremely jealous about what they thought was the social, economic and cultural progress made by the Harijans and particularly the Mahars and the Neo-Buddhists was evident from the following slogans they shouted while attacking the Mahars and the Neo-Buddhists and setting fire to their houses. "Why do you want to wear clothes better than ours? Why do you want houses built of bricks? Why do you want your children sent to schools and colleges?

M.B. Chitnis, a moderate Dalit intellectual wrote: "When one listens to the slogans of the perpetrators of atrocities as narrated by the victims, one is transposed to the days of the manusmriti........ all in tune with the duties that manusmriti prescribed for the untouchables. This was the ultimate social implication and result of the agitation sponsored by the urban intellectuals of Marathwada."[1]. A fortnight of violence left deep scars also in the minds of the Dalits in the other parts of the country. After the riots, when the Dalits took out protest marches, the slogans they shouted were: "Take back our citizenship; we have no mother land; casteists, keep your Hindustan to yourself; this social order has to be changed, we want to bring social revolution."[2]

The Dalit Panthers who were in favour of the change of name of the University decided on a programme to converge on Aurangabad on 6th December, 1979, the date of the Anniversary of the death of Dr. Ambedkar. They were to come from all over the country to change the name board of the University forcibly. They called this agitation the 'long march'. The march was banned by the authorities. The procession was intercepted by the police at several places. In spite of these steps, more than 20,000 people assembled at Aurangabad on 5th December, 1979 in addition to the locals who were in favour of a change in the name of the University. National leaders like Shri S.M. Joshi, the wife and son of the late Dr. Ambedkar also participated in the 'long march' and courted arrest.

The Mahars in Marathwada are a newly emerging group in a class spectrum ranging from the landless to middle class professionals. In each village, there are four to five Mahar graduates, mostly unemployed.

The caste tensions in rural Maharashtra continue in varying degree of intensity. One among the several reasons for this is the refusal by the Scheduled Castes to continue to perform unpleasant tasks including removal of carcasses and scavenging. In one such incident, reported from Akola district in January, 1985, the members of the Matang community refused to do scavenging jobs. The caste Hindus imposed a social boycott which resulted in depriving the Matang community of essential commodities. When this boycott failed to bring the Matang community to their knees, the Caste Hindus polluted the well which was the source of the drinking water for the Matangs.

The continuance of tension between the communities is in spite of some steps taken by the State Government to keep the differences from erupting into violence. Every district has a Committee called 'Dakshata' which meets every month to look into cases of differences between the caste Hindus and the Scheduled Castes. A special cell in the office of the Director General of Police deals with the complaints of Scheduled Castes and Scheduled Tribes. The general complaints of the police in resolving this matter is the delay in the disposal of cases at the level of the Courts. Unless the Criminal Justice System functions speedily, these complaints will not receive speedy disposal, which alone can make a significant dent in solving the problem.

References

1. S.P. Punalekar's paper: "Reflection on Violence in Maharashtra Region". He has quoted M.B. Chitnis.
2. IBID.

CHAPTER 17

KARNATAKA-POLITICS AS AN INSTRUMENT OF CHANGE

James Manor has observed[1] that the important point about caste dominance in Karnataka villages is that it tends to be less severe and oppressive in character than what exists in the villages of most of the other states of India...... The harshness of dominance is further mitigated by the fact that economic disparities between the rich and the poor have been less wide.

Devraj Urs who came to power in 1972 as the Chief Minister of Karnataka broke the dominance of the Vokaligas and Lingayats over the State politics without, at the same time, alienating them completely. He went further and made the groups which were until then considered as the disadvantaged ones, enjoy a higher degree of influence. It is not possible to say that any one socio-economic group is now dominant in State politics in Karnataka. "Some might wish to call this 'shared dominance' but in my view, when power is shared among so many groups, none can be said to be dominant."[2] Flowing from this, James Manor draws three important conclusions :

1) The coalition that Devraj Urs assembled is not only difficult but can easily be aborted;
2) The dominance of the landed groups (Lingayats and Vokaligas) at the village level remained unaffected despite the groups which were considered disadvataged exercising power in State politics for eight years;
3) The Vokaligas and Lingayats cannot expect to get back to their original level of dominance in State politics. This is because a large number of disadvantaged persons have also gained access to the bureaucracy at dif-

ferent levels and they can be expected to look after the interests of their groups within the Government.

Thus Karnataka can be said to have arrived at a level where conflicts between the different castes or different class within the same castes are not sharp. One perception of this is that they have arrived at a stage of greater equilibrium in the State and the types of violence by one caste group against another, which continue to be a common phenomenon particularly in the States of Uttar Pradesh and Bihar, are therefore seldom in evidence in Karnataka. This is a classic example of how astute political management affects the socio-economic factors in a manner which can reduce the level of violence as a concomitant of socio-economic change. In a sense, it also proves that at a particular stage of socio-economic change, caste factors can influence the complexion and direction of politics in a State. This pattern of development further holds out the promise that the weaker sections in some of the states can also hope to arrive at a level of socio-economic development comparable with the levels of similar groups in Karnataka. In short, Karnataka's experience proves the primacy of politics as an agent of peaceful change. Devraj Urs, during his office, with the co-operation of the disadvantaged groups implemented his policy of change gradually and in the process was able to introduce substantial reforms. The social disabilities that the Scheduled Castes have had to face in Karnataka have been much less than in other states.

Some of the factors that contributed to socio-economic transition stated by James Manor are : "Devraj Urs initiated schemes to provide houses for the poor, pensions for the aged, assistance in lean months to persons heavily dependent on labour, child development programmes for poor groups extending from the ante-natal stage to school going age, pressure to ensure that a large proportion of school-aged children from disadvantaged groups received some education, pressure on police to deal more evenly with vulnerable groups, pressure on employers to comply with the minimum wage law, initiatives to reduce rural indebtedness among the poor and to provide alternative sources of credit and the banning of performance of certain degrading tasks by the Scheduled Castes people. Urs also re-directed the flow of sizeable portion of political spoils towards the power groups. This was less widely advertised and less easily discernible than his new reformist programmes. But as Urs himself stated, it may have had as great an impact as all of them put together. In contrast to this, the conditions in Bihar have been put very succinctly by Francian Frankel: "Most Congress workers showed little sense of commitment to State development or to the welfare of Biharis that transcended loyalities to caste, community, kin-ship groups from which they were drawn. The party relied for success at the polls on caste leaders, who had large following in their own group and could also exploit patron-client ties."

Devraj Urs, in spite of the favour that he showed to the backward groups, did not either alienate or antagonise the Vokaligas or Lingayats. He listed the Vokaligas among backward classes eligible for special concessions from the Government. Devraj Urs played the game of patronage politics with consummate subtlety. He distributed patronage by creating opportunities for his rivals to enrich themselves as members of various Government Boards and Committees.

Devraj Urs was the architect of the Karnataka Land Reform Laws of 1974. The authenticity of his social concern was evident from the number of Land Tribunals he constituted, which at one stage stood at two hundred, at the rate of one for each taluk and even more than one in one taluk, if the pendency of applications seeking conferment of ownership rights to tenants warranted it. Devraj Urs sought to give practical shape to the concept of "Land to the Tiller" through the institution of Land Tribunals. The Tribunals were instructed to exercise their discretion in favour of the tenants as a matter of policy. Of the eight lakh applications filed before the Tritunals, more than three-fourths have been disposed of.

How significant and purposeful changes can be brought about in the socio-economic scene through the means of Institutional infrastructure devised for the purpose was more than amply demonstrated in Karnataka in the implementation of Land Reforms. This also proved that political leadership, when it is sincere and well-meaning can achieve results which would benefit the deprived and the depressed sections of society without provoking any serious social tensions and violence. Some of the safeguards provided in the implementation of the Land Reforms in Karnataka are : The tenants could pay up the occupancy price in a lump sum or in twenty years in annuities. Once the Land Tribunal granted occupancy rights, the civil court's jurisdiction did not extend to the decisions and orders of the Tribunals. The appearance of lawyers at any stage of the Tribunal's proceedings was barred. The only intervention permitted was an approach to the High Court through a writ petition under Article 226 or 227 of the Constitution on the ground of the order of the Tribunal being violative of natural justice. There was no appeal against the decision of the Tribunals which were quasi-judicial bodies

Since the non-official members of the Tribunals were drawn from the same taluks, it gave scope for the vested interests to influence events. But the Government could, on its own, initiate remedial action by removing the suspect member and reconstitute the Tribunal. Even so, that a few of the members of the Tribunals had misused their powers is evident from the fact that the High Court had passed severe strictures against them in their capacity as Tribunal members and who later happened to occupy important positions in public life. With all its failings and imperfections, the manner in which Land Reforms in Karnataka was implemented under Devraj Urs proves that with adequate safeguards and appropriate institutional infrastructure provisions at the administrative level, capable of responding to problems, social change can be brought about with minimum pain. That a responsive and an enlightened Government should keep such institutions in constant and continuous state of repair, review and even innovation is brought out by the decision of the present Government (1986) in Karnataka to set up District Appellate Tribunals to take charge of the problems arising from the decisions of the Land Tribunals at the taluka levels. This addition to the infrastructural arrangement was a direct sequel to the strictures that the Karnataka High Court passed against some of the decisions of the Land Tribunal, including the one in which one of the Ministers of the State Government was himself involved. The Minister resigned following the High Court judgement.

In spite of the foregoing rosy picture of the state of the society in Karnataka, it would be wrong to conclude that there are no flaws in this respect in the State, It has also its share of maladministration and corruption, which in turn generate the kind of concealed violence in the form of injustice and affront to human dignity. According to a report the programme for release and rehabilitation of bonded labour in Karnataka was looked into by the Public Accounts Committee of the State Legilature. It had noticed several irregularities which point to certain very disturbing trends. According to the report presented to the State Assembly in July, 1985, rehabilitation scheme had been sanctioned only to half of the 62,000 workers identified as in bondage and released thereafter while the number actually provided with gainful employment worked out to hardly 30%. In monetary terms, utilization was less than 65% of the sanctioned amount. It has been alleged that there is a nexus between bureaucratic minions and the middlemen who were responsible for misappropriation of funds. That they could set up bogus beneficiaries and hire milch cattle for a day to enact a rehabilitation drama was a reflection on the integrity of the administration. The P.A.C. had observed that the State Government had to initiate measures to make the watch dog panels function well.

Untouchability is very much alive in Karnataka, though the disputes arising between the Harijans and caste Hindus is handled promptly by the Police which prevents these incidents from assuming more serious dimensions. Further, according to the staement of the Home Minister of the State, the Superintendent of Police of the District is held responsible personally for the safety of the Harijans. The Superintendents of Police usually visit the spots of trouble and ensure appropriate action against the offenders. This has certainly helped in keeping the violence down to the minimum.

If the incidents of violence on account of caste tensions is less in Karnataka, it has much to do with better political management of the State by Devraj Urs during the 1970s and the traditional arrangement that were inherited from the princely State of Mysore. Even so, untouchability is a fact of life though it continues without much overt violence. But even the extent to which it is practised should be treated as violence to the feelings of the victims. This is an area where new institutional safeguards need to be devised as the existing ones have failed to eradicate the evil. This observation is valid for most States in the country.

References

1. James Manor: "Caste, Class, dominance and Politics in a cohesive society" (1984).
2. IBID.

CHAPTER 18

GUJARAT
THE THREE AGITATIONS OF 1974, 1981 AND 1985

The caste composition of the population of Gujarat is as followings :

Brahmins	4.06%
Vanias	2.96%
Rajputs	4.85%
Patidars (Patels)	12.16%
Kolis (Kshatriyas)	24.22%
Scheduled Castes	7.17%
Scheduled Tribes	17.6%
Muslims	8.53%

Kolis form the largest class cluster in Gujarat. They call themselves Kshatriyas. The Kolis (Kshatriyas) are different from the Rajputs.

The improvement registered by the Scheduled Castes of Gujarat in the field of education has been appreciable. The Scheduled Castes and the Scheduled Tribes have certainly availed of the facilities extended by the Government for education as could be seen from Annexures F-1, F-2,.F and F-3. The Scheduled Castes have a literacy rate of 30.7% which is second only to Kerala which has 55.9% literacy. The Scheduled Caste urban population in Gujarat is also the highest among all the States, being 27.2%. The greater mobility of the Scheduled Castes has certainly affected the available opportunities of employment which are becoming increasingly scarce.

The Scheduled Castes of Gujarat traditionally suffer from several disabilities. Untouchability continues to be practised in several villages. Access to temples, houses and shops is not permitted. There are separate sources of water supply. Even so, the Scheduled Castes have begun to assert themselves. In the village Golana in Khera district the Harijans antagonised the local Rajputs by forming cooperatives of their own. In the resultant clash, 4 Harijans were shot dead and several injured on 25th January, 1986. From far and near in the State, Harijans converged on the village to show their solidarity. When the Chief Minister visited the village on the Republic Day, he was presented with a memorandum which read : "Are we citizens of this country ? If we are, we want to be allowed to live with dignity. We want nobody's pity. We just want our rights."

In the first two decades following independence, members of the dominant caste such as the Vanias, the Patels and the Brahmins, derived maximum benefits from the various developmental programmes. It is only since then that the Scheduled Castes, the Scheduled Tribes and the other Backward Castes have come to avail themselves of the benefits. Even then they are quite far from enjoying their full share of the legitimate entitlements arising out of the reservations policy.

The size of the urban middle class in Gujarat employed in industries, in public and private sectors, urban centres, petty-business and small-scale industries has increased in recent years. Exact statistical data are not available. According to an estimate workers employed in organized and unorganized sectors have increased from 8.9 lakhs in 1966 to 14 lakhs in 1982. A large part of them consist of Vanias, Brahmins and Patidars. There are also a number of Scheduled Castes, Scheduled Tribes and Other Backward Castes (OBCs), though their proportion is small. Between 1978 and 1984 the number of unemployed persons registered in employment exchanges in Gujarat had almost doubled : 3,97,000 in 1978 to 6,31,800 in 1984. Among the unemployed persons, as many as 59% were educated. The middle class of the upper and the middle castes were adversely affected by the rise in the number of educated unemployed. This was attributed to the policy of reservation followed by the Government. The "roster system" in government jobs further accelerated the chances of upward mobility to the Scheduled Castes and the Scheduled Tribes as against the upper and the middle castes who had to bide their time for promotion. It is not unusual for Scheduled Castes and Scheduled Tribes employees trained by the upper caste senior employees to rise above these senior officers themselves within a short time thereby giving rise to jealousy and heartburn among those who are left behind. The impact of this was evident in the agitations of 1981 and 1985. While the 1974 agitation launched by the Navnirman Samiti was spearheaded by the middle class drawn from all castes, the anti-reservation agitations of 1980-81 and 1985 were by the middle class drawn from the upper and the intermediate castes.

Gujarat has seen three important agitations between 1974 and 1985. The circumstances which precipitated the crisis of 1974 were steep price rise and scarcity conditions. It was alleged in the Vidhan Sabha and outside that corruption was responsible for the high market price of edible Oil in Gujarat. P.N. sheth[1] has referred to the rise in the mess bill of the middle class students in the hostels which was attributed to maladministration and corruption. A series of Bandhs were followed by Gujarat Bandh on 26th January, 1974 when 43 towns and cities, spread over two thirds of the State, came under curfew for 37 hours. There were open clashes between the police and the people. Six people were killed in the firing that took place. The Republic Day was not celebrated in Gujarat in 1974. Students, teachers and lawyers, participated in the agitations. The agitation led to the resignation of the Chief Minister, followed by the dissolution of the Assembly.

This was the first agitation of its kind organised without any political party initiating or guiding and controlling its course. This is, however, not to say that the political parties derived no mileage from the agitation. This agitation was also unique in the sense that it transcended caste and class barriers. The middle classes of all castes, and communities participated in the agitation. Yet another unique feature was that owing to the circumstances under which the then Chief Minister of Gujarat, Chimanbhai Patel, had come to power, he had antagonised party authorities at the Centre which also indirectly fuelled the agitation which eventually brought the Ministry down. The Centre had pressurised the Gujarat Government by a steady reduction in the supply of wheat and rice to Gujarat and also by refusing prmission to the State Government to purchase foodgrains from Punjab and Haryana. As against this, the Central allocation of foodgrain was stepped up month by month after the resignation of the Ministry. This provides a new dimension to violence as a by-product of the faction fight within the ruling party. This phenomenon, though not very frequent deserves to be watched in the country in future.

The agitation of 1980-1981 was the direct outcome of the reservation issue. The middle classes belonging to the upper castes, namely, Brahmins, Patidars, Vanias and others were responsible for launching the agitation in December, 1980 against the policy of reservation of seats in the post-graduate studies in Medicine. The agitation continued for three months. Clashes broke out between the students and others of the Scheduled Castes and Scheduled Tribes on the one side and those belonging to the upper castes on the other. Though reservation was not abolished, the Government gave certain concessions to the agitating medical students, who had initially launched the agitation against the reservation of seats. In this agitation the middle class got split between those belonging to the upper castes and the backward castes. This is in sharp contrast to the 1974 agitation when the entire middle class spectrum cutting across caste lines had combined to bring down the Government. In the agitation of 1980-1981, the huts of the Scheduled Castes were set on fire and they were beaten up in the rural areas of Ahmedabad and Surendranagar districts. More than a dozen Harijans lost their lives. Between mid-April and mid-May, 1981, about 700 Dalit families in Ahmedabad embraced Buddhism. According to Babal Bhai Mehta and his band of Sarvodaya workers who toured 29 villages of Central Gujarat in April

1981 the Harijans in the villages were harassed and discriminated against for employment by upper caste farmers. Even the mill workers of Ahmedabad split into Dalit Hitraksha Samiti and Sawarna Hitraksha Samiti. This was indeed a body blow to the Mazdoor Mahajan Trade Union started by Gandhiji 60 years ago and which had more than 3 lakh mill workers as its members.

On the basis of the Baxi Committee report, the State Government had provided for 10% reservation to the Other Backward Castes. This was sought to be raised by another 18% on the basis of the Rane Commission's report in January, 1985. Though the Rane Commission had rejected caste as a measurement of backwardness, the Government rejected the major recommendation of the Commission which dealt with income as the yardstick of backwardness, while accepting the recommendation of the reservation quota. That this announcement of an increase in the reservation quota was more a gimmick to derive political mileage in the Assembly elections that was imminent is evident from the actual use that had been made of even the existing reservation. The table below is self-explanatory:

UTILIZATION

class	Reservation	Year	Percentage availed	
			Medical	Engineering
	%			
Scheduled Castes	7	1983-1984	6.5	6.6
Scheduled Castes		1984-1985	6.4	6.5
Scheduled Tribes	14	1983-1984	5.8	3.46
Scheduled Tribes		1984-1985	3.4	4.5
Other Backward Castes	10	1983-1984	5.0	4.05
Other Backward Castes		1984-1985	3.5	6.16

The immediate provocation for the 1985 agitation was the statement made by Gujarat Government to increase the quota of reservation for the backward castes from 10 to 28 per cent. Without minimising the contribution of the anti-reservationists in promoting and continuing the agitation of 1985, it needs to be pointed out that the agitation took the course that it did bacause of several extraneous factors. An important factor was the dissidence within the ruling party. The elements who had wielded power earlier and who found themselves suddenly out of the Ministry had their own axes to grind in giving the agitation an extra edge of vandalism and what was worse, a communal turn. The dissident elements in the ruling party apparently wanted to settle their political scores with the Chief Minister who had the temerity not to include them in his Cabinet. Though the events that shook Ahmedabad for more than five months from February 1985 onwards may have had their origin in certain tangible and identifiable reasons, soon these took courses which could not be controlled. This was largely because of the impact of several imponderable factors arising out of the political ambition and greed of individuals and groups who exploited the situation to derive personal and group benefits.

The three-member fact-finding team of the Editor's Guild which visited Ahmedabad during the agitation of 1985 concluded that the agitation had been the creation of politicians. According to the report of the team[2] : "The Chief Minister...... himself played politics when just before the State Assembly poll he announced an additional 18 per cent reservation for the backward castes. This was only a ploy to attract votes because the Chief Minister took no steps to implement his announcement..... The misuse of the police for party or political ends has implied an erosion of discipline in the police force of Gujarat." The team also found some substance in the allegation that the communal riots had been engineered at some level of the Government to divert the attention from caste conflicts and the anti-reservation agitation.

In both the 1981 and 1985 agitations the middle classes of the upper castes had an edge ove the middle classes of the Scheduled Castes and the Scheduled Tribes in terms of their size, their unity and their resources. As against this, the middle classes of the backward castes, Scheduled Castes and

Scheduled Tribes were alienated from their caste fellows who were poor and were not hopeful of getting any advantage out of the reservation policy in their life time. Therefore, the bottom strata of the backward castes, the Scheduled Castes and the Scheduled Tribes were indifferent to the agitation. This is a very important and significant feature. Though caste has its attraction in promoting a distinct and separate identity of the people of that group, apparently it is not capable of transcending the economic disparties between varying degrees of economic affluence within the same group, save in exceptional circumstances.

The politics of Gujarat has brought into being a new alignment of castes and communities which if repeated in other States is likely to affect the course and complexion of the pattern of life in these states. To counter the move of the Patels, who swung from the Congress to the Janta Party in 1975, one of the political leaders of Gujarat conceived the strategy of combining Kshatriyas, Harijans, Adivasis and the Muslims into what came to be called as the KHAM.

In the 1985 assembly poll out of the 149 Congress MLAs in Gujarat, 100 belonged to KHAM and OBCs (Other Backward Castes). The upper castes found themselves in danger of losing political power which had slipped out of their hands and into the hands of backward castes, even while they continued to dominate the economic scene in the state. For once, the political haves of yesterday have become the have nots of today and vice versa in Gujarat.

The caste war in Gujarat came once again to the sufrace in a violent form with the sudden assertion of the agriculturists on a wide scale in March, 1987. This disrupted life completely in many districts and a few people were killed in police firing in Ahmedabad. One cause of this assertion by the intermediate caste led by the patidars was as much economic as political. In a way the farmers' agitation of 1987 was the rural version of the anti-reservation agitation staged in 1985 in the urban centres of Gujarat. Whatever hopes the

Patidar led intermediate castes had of regaining the earlier dominance were belied by the congress victories of the KHAM in the district and taluk panchayat poll held in January, 1987. In the 1985 Assembly elections the congress party had garnered 55.54% of votes. Its share at the district level in the Panchayat poll came down to 50.77% and at the taluka level to a still lower 47.75%. This was an indication that the intermediate caste cannot be written off at the local level.[3]

Whether or not the two groups, one of which has the political power while the other continued to command the economic resources are able to arrive at a peaceful and harmonious relationship, is the point at issue. On the answer to this will depend whether the public life of Gujarat will be marked by peace or by endemic violence.

Even though the anti-reservation agitators had won a point which would certainly have a serious impact on the backward castes, it cannot be said that the last has been heard or said on the subjet. To the extent that the accord between the agitators and the Government had no relevance to the intrinsic merits of the case, the accord could also be upset by yet another agitation if mounted with the same sustained vigour by those who are affected adversely by the accord. The anti-reservation agitation found its reaction among the backward castes and the tribals when they demonstrated their strength by taking out an impressive procession estimated at 1.5 Kilometer long in August, 1985. They warned the Government against the termination of the roster system. The Press also played the role of a catalyst in fuelling the agitation of 1985 and came under very severe attack both from the police and the pro-reservationists.

The Gujarat agitation of 1985 lasted for 150 days, during which more than 215 lives were sacrificed. The loss to business and industry was estimated at more than Rs. 2,200/- crores. The loss and the inconvenience suffered by the students was an additional cost.

References

1. P.N. Sheth : "Political Change in India" (1977).
2. Report of the Editors' Guild on the riots in ahmedabad (1985).
3. Times of India, Lucknow dated March 24, 1987.

CHAPTER 19

RESERVATION AS AN ISSUE

As of now the country has had only the first dose of violence in Gujarat on the issue of reservation. The Mandal Commission report on the subject of reservation is still to be considered by the State Governments. Whether or not it is implemented, its recommendations have the potential for violence. In the meantime public opinion is being built up in favour of its implementation in Uttar Pradesh. A massive procession was taken out by the people of all the Backward communities, including Scheduled Castes, in Lucknow in December, 1986 demanding its early implementation. How and when this peaceful demand will degenerate into violence and intercaste conflict remains to be seen. But the trends are ominous.

That the Uttar Pradesh Government has views on reservation which are different from those of some other State Governments which have been referred to here is evident from its communication to the Centre in 1983. An extract from the communication is reproduced below :

"To use backward class and backward castes as mutually exchangeable is neither rational nor fair...... It is time to examine carefully the appropriateness and the adequacy of measures adopted so far by the various states to improve the conditions of the socially and educationally backward classes. The nation's responsibility towards them does not end with reservation in jobs. Such measures may not produce any significant difference in the lives of the vast majority of the socially oppressed and deprived sections of the community. Bolder and more radical measures are needed to create an equitable and just social system."[1]

In Karnataka, the Second Backward Classes Commission chaired by Shi T. Venkataswamy had been appointed in April, 1983 by the Janata Chief Minister, Ramakrishna Hedge to review the existing reservation policy in that State. The Commission recommended a reduction in the number of beneficiary communities and caste groups and in the percentage of reservation as a whole. The total reservations recommended excluding the Scheduled Castes and Scheduled Tribes dropped from the existing 50% to 27%. The Vokkaligas who had been brought within the benefit of reservation by Devraj Urs were dropped in the new list. This led to an agitation. The Hegde Government's reaction to the agitation was to reject the Venkataswamy Commission's report completely and issue a Government order which would remain valid for three years. During this period of three years, yet another Commission would give its report setting out more precise guidelines for reservation. The net result of the Hegde Government's policy on reservation is that both the Vokkaligas and the Lingayats have been brought within the ambit of the reservation though the benefit of it will be confined to the categories who come within different income limits depending upon their caste. According to one estimate, 89% of the State's population are now eligible for reservation in educational institutions and 92% for government jobs, subject to an income limit of Rs. 10,000/- per annum.

It is difficult to resist the conclusion that by rejecting the Venkataswamy Commission's report totally the Karnataka Government was plumbing more for short term political gains than for long term resolution of the traditional caste rivalries. In spite of some of its faults, the Venkataswamy Commission's report was the first serious attempt made in independent India to take account of the mobility of castes and classes and determine backwardness on the basis of actual house-to-house surveys.

The Government of Karnataka have brought out a blue jacket publication which is in the nature of a defence of the

Government's controversial scheme of reservation for the Backward classes, superseding the report of the Venkataswamy Commission. "The document argues that the new policy maintained the total percentage of resrevation at the same level as before (68%). It maintained that castes and communities had been categorised under five different groups to ensure that the advanced groups among the backward classes did not corner all the benefits. With the income ceiling taken into account, 55% to 60% of the population would be entitled to benefits under Article 15 (4) and 16 (4) of the Constitution".[2]

The fact that the two dominant communities such as the Vokkaligas and Lingayats wanted to be included within the privileged groups inspite of the progress that they have made in the educational and social fields is indicative of the trend that reservation as a policy is going to be with us for a very long time to come with unpredictable consequences, all of which may not be conductive to peace in the country.

It would be worthwhile to read the latest order of the Karnataka Government on the subject of reservation in the context of the judgement of the Supreme Court delivered in the case of R. Balaji Vs. State of Mysore (Gajendragadkar J) AIR 1963 Supreme Court 649 (V 50 C 101) 28th September, 1962. The Bench consisted of B.P. Sinha, C.J., P.B. Gajendragadkar, K.N. Wanchoo, K.C. Das Gupta and J.C. Shah, J.J. The judgement established certain very important principles which continue to be valid even to-day. The principles or the policy guidelines enunciated by the Karnataka Government in its recent order cannot be said to be consistent with the judgement as the extracts reproduced below will show.[3]

"The backward classes for whose improvement special provision is contemplated by Article 15 (4) are in the matter of their backwardness comparable to Scheduled Castes and Scheduled Tribes..... The backwardness is not either social or educational, but it is both social and educational....... Special provision is contemplated for classes of citizens and not for individual citizens as such and so, though the caste of the group of citizens may be relevant, its importance should not be exaggerated. If the classification of backward classes of citizens was based solely on the caste of the citizens it may not always be logical and may perhaps contain the vice of perpetuating the cates themselves.

2) "If the caste of the group of citizens was made the sole basis for determining the social backwardness of the said group, that test would inevitably breakdown in relation to many sections of Indian society which do not recognise caste in the conventional sense known to Hindu society. How is one going to decide whether Muslims, Christians or Jains or even Lingayats are socially backward or not?..... Though caste in relation to Hindus may be a relevant factor to consider in determining the social backwardness of groups or classes of citizens, it cannot be made the sole or the dominant test in that behalf. Social backwardness is in the ultimate analysis the result of poverty to a very large extent.

3) "Class of citizens whose average of student population was the same or just below state average cannot be treated as educationally backward...... It is only communities which are well below the state average that could properly be regarded as educationally backward classes of citizens.

4) "It would be extremely unreasonable to assume that in enacting Article 15 (4), the Constitution intended to provide that where the advancement of the backward classes or the Scheduled Castes and Tribes was concerned the fundamental rights of the citizens which constitute the rest of the society were to be completely and absolutely ignored...... The interest of the weaker sections of society..... have tobe adjusted with the interest of the community as a whole.

5) "Speaking generally and in a broad way a special provision should be less than 50%, how much less than 50%

would depend upon the relevant prevailing circumstances in each case."

6) "On 31st July, 1962 the State passed the impugned order which supersedes all previous orders. Under this order, the backward classes are divided into two categories :

1) Backward Classes and
2) More Backward Classes.

The effect of this order is that 28% is reserved for backward classes so-called and 22% for more backward classes. The reservation of 15% and 3% for the Scheduled Castes and Scheduled Tribes respectively continues to be the same. The result of this order is that 68% of the seats for technical colleges is reserved..... It is necessary to add that the sub-classification made by the order, between backward classes and more backward classes does not appear to be justified under Article 15 (4).... in introducing two categories of backward classes what the impugned order, in substance, purports to do is to devise measures for the benefit of all the classes of citizens who are less advanced compared to the most advanced classes in the State and that, in our opinion, is not the scope of Article 15 (4)... Classification of the two categories therefore is not warranted by Article 15 (4).

7) "It would cause grave prejudice to national interest if considerations of merit are completely excluded by wholesale reservation of seats in all technical institutions. Therefore, consideration of national interest and the interest of the community or society as a whole cannot be ignored in determining the question as to whether the special provision contemplated by Article 15 (4) can exclude the rest of the society altogether.

8) "The impugned order in the present case has categorised the backward classes on the sole basis of caste which in our opinion is not permitted by Article 15 (4); and we have also held that the reservation of 68% made by the impugned order is plainly inconsistent with the concept of the special provision authorised by Article 15 (4). Therefore, it follows

that the impugned order is a fraud on the Constitutional power conferred on the State by Article 15 (4)."

The Andhra Pradesh Government issued in July 1986 an order increasing the Backward Classes' quota of reservation in jobs and college seats from 25% to 44%. This order apparently was a shrewd political move by the Telugu Desam Government to forestall a likely move by the Congress party to exploit the reservation issue for political purposes. The Government's order was followed by a Statewide agitation by the anti-reservationists which lasted six weeks when the High Court set aside the order. In a judgement delivered on September 5, 1986 a full bench of the Andhra Pradesh High Court held that the State Government's order enhancing the backward castes quota of reservation in jobs and college seats was unconstitutional. The reaction to this judgement among the backward caste youth was understandable. But their agitation to protest against the judgement did not take off.

Both in Gujarat and in Andhra Pradesh the anti-reservationists were able to have their way. This is accounted for by the fact that while in Gujarat the Government certainly gave in to the pressure from the economically affluent communities, in Andhra Pradesh the judiciary came to the rescue of the anti-reservationists. In a sense, the High Court judgement came as a relief to the Government who in any case may have eventually succumbed to the pressures of those who enjoyed both economic and political power.

The concept of reservation is referred to as the policy of positive discrimination by the American judiciary. Their judgements on this concept present a point of view which is relevant in the overall concept of justice and equity. Hence they are referred to here.

In a case of positive discrimination reported from the Supreme Court of the United States of America, Justice Douglas, in his dissenting judgement had observed : "There is no superior person by constitutional standards. Defunis who is White is entitled to no advantage by reason of that fact; Nor is he subject to any disability, no matter what his race or colour. Whatever his race is, he has a constitutional right to have his application considered on its individual merit in a rational and neutral manner. A segregated admission process creates suggestions of stigma and caste no less than a segregated class room and in the end it may produce that result despite its contrary intentions. One other assumption must be clearly disapproved that Blacks or Browns cannot make it on their individual merit. This is a stamp of inferiority that a State is not permitted to place on any Lawyer". Defunis was a White applicant for a Law School and despite the fact that he had higher marks, a Black applicant was preferred to Defunis, apparently in an effort to give an impression of fair representation to the Blacks in the School admissions.

In another important case of positive discrimination reported from the United States of America, Allan Bakke, a White candidate was denied admission to a Medical School even though he had higher marks than the Black who had secured admission. Four Judges ruled the special programme as violative of equality, while four others upheld it. So the decisive opinion was of the 9th Judge, Mr. Justice Powell. Justice Powell while generally approving of the legitimacy of the preferential process ruled that "there is a measure of iniquity in forcing innocent persons in respondent's (Allan Bakke) position to bear the burden of redressing grievances not of their making."

Thus, on the subject of reservation what so far has triumphed in the three States of Gujarat, Andhra Pradesh and Karnataka as a result of the agitations mounted by the pro and anti-reservationists, is not the principle of reservation in its basic desirability and rationality as a means to usher in a society based on social justice, but in effect, the volume and violence of pressure mounted by the more articulate and influential among the communities whose perception of the concept of reservation is vastly different from the national policy imperatives of the Government and the basic requirements of the backward communities. The issue of reservation in the very nature of it is extremely sensitive without our having to make it more so by using it as a tool of political expediency. As events have turned out we are tending to vest the concept of reservation with a political character which it should not have. The only sound reason for resorting to it is socio-economic considerations. By giving it a political dimension, we are not only undermining the strength and stability of the political process of an infant democracy but are also implanting violence in the soil, which will plague us for years to come.

References

1. The extract of the State Government letter addressed to the Centre quoted by N.C. Saxena and Imtiaz Ahmed in their paper: "Caste, Land and Political Power in Uttar Pradesh. (1984).
2. The Hindu, a national daily, Dt. 7th December, 1986.
3. Judgement of the Supreme Court in the case of R. Balaji Vs. State of Mysore (Gajendragadkar J) A.I.R. 1963 Supreme Court 649 (V 50 C 101) (1986).

PART V

CHAPTER 20

CONCLUSION AND POLICY IMPLICATIONS

In the course of this study, I have not uncovered any startling truths. I have not propounded any profound theories. I have offered no simple solution to the several difficult problems. I have merely attempted to catalogue a few specific instances from the field on the basis of which certain simple conclusions have been drawn. They are worth taking note of, and being acted upon, if we are to develop as a secular, egalitarian and sound democracy.

Some of the broad conclusions that emerge from this study are:

A democratic Government rules not so much by the continuous use of power as by the social sanction behind its authority; but this authority will not be effective at the level of the people if the Government exercising it falls short of the basic moral character which is what ultimately vests a government with legitimacy. The manner in which the Gujarat Government used the reservation issue, more as a ploy to derive political advantage rather than as a matter of genuine concern for the welfare of the backward castes and groups raised certain very valid and serious doubts regarding the intentions behind the Government's decisions. To that extent, the moral authority of the Government suffered a demonstrable damage. This in no small measure contributed to the equivocation and prevarication which characterised the handling of the agitation by the Government, and that in turn contributed to the duration and the intensity of violence.

Both in 1974 and in 1985 Gujarat demonstrated that if the Government's stand on basic issues is not based on reason and justice a political party having a majority in the Legislature by itself would be of little avail in sustaining a particular council of Ministers in power. In a democratic dispensation, it is usually the practice, and the right of political parties to spearhead agitations to ventilate popular demands. The agitations of 1974, 1981 and 1985 were however launched and seen through successfully not by political parties but by individuals and groups many of whom did not have any political affiliation. This is, however, not to suggest that the political party leaders of different pursuasions did not jump on the bandwagon as and when they found the going good. These agitations amply demonstrated that non-institutionalised politics can be successfully played in a limited way when the issues inolved. have the support of large sections of the people.

In a democracy the people cannot be taken for granted and decisions that affect the interests of large segments of the population cannot be taken lightheartedly on grounds of political expediency. This is particularly so when the Government has to deal with people who are educated, enlightened and forward-looking and have the capacity to organize themselves at short notice. The people of Gujarat have proved that agitations pay even though in the process the people have to pay a very heavy price.

The successive agitations in Gujarat in 1974, 1981 and again in 1985 pose a serious dilemma which all serious students of public affairs have to face, and on the issue involved arrive at some workable conclusions. Judged by the eventual outcome of each one of these agitations, do we condemn or condone the agitational methods employed in spite of the violence that was integral to each one of these agitations? Unless the dilemma is resolved rationally in the context of securing justice as people see it, it would seem that violence will continue to have relevance in the scheme of things. Contexts such as these seem to give relevance and renewal to the use of violence in human affairs and reinforce the belief of the people that violence per se should not be rejected out of hand. Only the future will reveal whether the results achieved through such agitations will be reckoned as milestones of progress or signposts of disintegration.

The situation in which Gujarat finds itself today is the inevitable product of the political games that the politicians have often played in their anxiety to retain individuals or groups in political power. Castes and communities have merely been pawns in this game of exploitation by politicians. Considered in this context one cannot help feeling that politics played by unscrupulous politicians can sharpen cleavages and aggravate caste tensions. It is only when politics is used as a tool to bring about socio-economic changes smoothly instead of being used to further divide a society which already stands severely fragmented that we are likely to prevent the perniciousness of caste conflicts.

When the ruling party is riven with internal factions, and is organisationally not strong enough to enforce discipline, one or the other faction exploits a given situation to discredit the faction in power. In doing so, it is not concerned with the contribution that it is making to aggravate a situation which is already marked by violence. This is what happened in Gujarat in 1974 and again in 1985. Though both these agitations started on certain identifiable issues and causes, they were aggravated by the induction of factors which were totally extraneous to the initial causes. In 1974 the circumstances under which the Chief Minister had manoeuvred himself into power did not have the blessings of the Central authority of the party. Hence the Centre was as much interested in the downfall of the

Ministry as those who had initiated the agitation on the issues of price rise and corruption. Similarly the 1985 agitation started by the anti-reservationists got entangled with the dissidence within the ruling party. Even the communal turn that the agitation took was reported to have been given by a dissident within the ruling party who did not find a place in the Cabinet. This form of violence in public life arising out of the infighting within the party bodes ill for democratic norms and values. Instead of putting politics to work as an honest agent of change, if it is played by whichever party happens to be in power as an exercise in faction fights and settling scores between groups within the same party, it can create conditions which can eventually have a severe destabilising effect on the country as a whole. A democracy cannot afford to set such precedents if the democratic institutions are at all to survive.

Divergence of political power from economic dominance is becoming a fact of life in Gujarat. All the sources of economic power such as trade, industry, and the co-operative sector, among others, continue to be dominated by the Patels, Vanias, Rajputs and Brahmins. Though the kshatriyas, Scheduled Castes, Scheduled Tribes and the Other Backward Castes have increasingly come to have a greater share in their political power, they have not been able to improve their economic power correspondingly. The conflicts between the wielders of economic and political power have led to clashes between communities resulting in murders particularly in Saurashtra. The areas over which the Kshatriyas and the weaker sections have a say are limited to Government jobs and welfare programmes and as of now have not extended to the dispensing of economic patronage. But if the growth of political power continues according to the trends that are now visible, one expects that over a period of time it is bound to affect the economic dominance of the upper castes also. That will not fail to generate a degree of violence though it is difficult to speculate on the nature and extent of it at this stage

The agitations in Gujarat have raised yet another important issue on the answer to which will depend the relevance of violence in a democratic set up. The issue is: does public opinion always reflect faithfully public interest, and are the two co-terminous? If they are not, where does one begin and the other end? Unlike the outcome of the 1974 Navnirman agitation, in the light of the results of the 1985 agitation in Gujarat, it can be stated that the public opinion as asserted by one section of the population was not co-terminous with the wider public interest, that is, the interest of the State of Gujarat as a whole.

Certain features have characterised the silent resentment or the open agitation triggered off by the reservation policy of the Gujarat and Andhra Pradesh Government. Some of these are: the agitations were led by the youth who refuse to be discriminated against for what their forefathers did or did not do to the weaker sections of the community in the centuries gone by. The basic issue is: Should past victimisation automatically result in disability to the successors of those who had been responsible for the victimisation, regardless of their present socio-economic condition? Assuming that positive discrimination is a step in the right direction to help the emancipation of the weaker sections, should this not be applied in a manner which will provide benefit to the maximum number of the weaker sections? Will this be achieved by the application of the policy that is being followed at present?

Reservation as a panacea for ameliorating the backwardness of the weaker sections, and as an atonement for the sign of centuries-old discrimination cannot be taken beyond a point without serious damage to the social fabric. This will throw up its own contradictions and complexities as it has already begun to. The advantage of reservation is that the weaker sections compete among themselves and not with those belonging to the castes who are referred to as the dominant ones and hence, supposedly stronger. If the assumption that competition between the economically stronger and the weaker sections is an unequal exercise is valid, we have already arrived at a stage when the competition even between the weaker sections themselves has become one between those of the weaker section who are economically stronger and those who continue to be economically deprived and depressed. Can it be said that the children of All India Service Officers belonging to the weaker section are on the same footing as the children of parents who have not yet come by the benefits of reservation even marginally? If therefore, competition between economically unequal sections is an unequal competition how can we make it a fairer competition unless those of the weaker sections who have had the benefits of the reservation for one or two generations and who have attained an economic status above a stipulated level are not in effect de-scheduled', leaving the weakest among the weaker sections to avail of the benefits of reservation? In the process of eliminating one set of inequalities we have to guard against ushering in another set of inequalities.

Positive discrimination being a means to an end, ought to be so employed as to ensure that while if affords full protection to the disadvantaged, it does not become amenable to any type of misuse by the privileged few among the weaker sections. In this context the roster system as it is operating in some of the States, apart from making serious inroads into administrative efficiency, holds the potential for serious indiscipline and unrest in the Services. This system needs to be suitably regulated so as to ensure that those who are entitled to reservation for initial entry into Services are also not enabled to go up the ladder far too prematurely but only after a minimum number of years at each of the levels.

The policy of positive discrimination has run into rough weather in several States. It needs to be made clear that the reservation provided for the Scheduled Castes and the Scheduled Tribes is not what is resented by those who are outside the benefit of reservations. They resent the increasing reservations that are being made for what have come to be referred to as the backward castes. This is because the policy of reservation for the backward castes cannot be given effect to without correspondingly reducing the opportunities available for the forward castes. "It is at this point that the tension between equality as a policy and as a right is most clearly revealed, for it is difficult to create and maintain on a large scale special opportunities for some without eating into the equal opportuniteis of all[1]." The people generally concede that the State should do more for those who are disadvantaged. But the criteria of deciding who are he disadvantaged should be based not on caste but on economic consideration. It is the scale of reservation extending up and down the line among the backward castes that is being resented. The programme of reservation has created a vested interest in backwardness as should be evident from the Karnataka experience in the context of the Venkataswamy commission report. Since the backward communities are getting increasingly organized on political lines, the policy of reservation has become functionally a means of political consolidation. A political process based and conditioned on caste identities carries with it the seeds of insidious political fragmentation which can be a source of serious threat to democratic stability. In a scheme of things where caste quotas of reservation for jobs and for seats in educational institutions keep increasing, personal merit and ability is grossly at a discount. A situation in which everyone who has been denied access to a position of responsibility even though he is better qualified on merit compared to the one who has been accommodated simply by virtue of his being a member of a particular community is not going to be conducive to peace. Conflict and violence are inherent in such a situation. It is indeed an irony that the policy of reservation instead of weakening the caste hierarchy which has been the largest single bane of this country is tending to reinforce and perpetuate this evil.

The 1990 election will be a water-shed in the democratic experiment of our country. This is because one of the issues which will have to figure prominently in the election manifesto of the different political parties would have to be whether or not the reservation of seats for Scheduled Castes and Scheduled Tribes in Parliament and State Assemblies should continue beyond 1990, and as a sequel to that or even independent of it, reservation in Services should continue. While Article 334 of the Constitution provides a time limit of forty years from the commencement of the Constitution for reservation of seats in Parliament and State Assemblies, there is no such limitation as far as reservation for jobs is concerned. This is however without prejudice to Article 330 of the Constitution which provides for reservation of seats in the Parliament and the Assemblies for the Scheduled Tribes in Nagaland, Meghalaya, Arunachal Pradesh and in Mizoram. The relevant figures for reservation for these four States will be based on the 1971 census which will continue till the first Census after 2000 A.D. according to the Proviso to Article 330 introduced in 1976 and the Constitution 51st amendment act of 1985.

Extension of the reservation in jobs beyond 1990 is likely to provoke a far more serious confrontation. The seeds have already been sown in Gujarat, and the resulting trends are evident. While there may be demands from the upper castes for terminating it or even for modifying it by de-scheduling those who have gone above a certain economic level, the scheduled castes and tribes are sure to ask for its continuance, and justifiably too as the bulk of them would not have had even the first generational benefits of the decades of reservation because of its failure to percolate down to large groups among them. If those who are economically well off among the weaker sections refuse to be descheduled, this will inevitably give rise to complications.

In the State of Bihar and in some parts of Uttar

Pradesh such violence as have disfigured the State scenes have largely been the outcome of the resistance offered by the vested interests to the process of socio-economic changes initiated by the State through Agrarian Reforms, developmental programmes and anti-poverty projects. This is however not to suggest that the Scheduled Castes have always been at the receiving end of violence. They have also responded with violence in varying degrees in the process of trying to overcome the resistance from the vested interests to the realization of their legitimate rights. The intermediate castes who belong to the backward group happened to be the traditional cultivators and on that account became the immediate beneficiaries of the abolition of Zamindari. The new found accretion to their economic power has also conferred on them additional political power. Yet their attitude to the weaker sections has not been any more helpful and sympathetic compared to the attitude of the traditionally dominant castes towards these sections at the bottom of the socio-economic ladder. If anything, they also have been as much resistant to change as the earlier vested interests. In fact, they have become a new class of vested interests. In effect the States of Bihar and Uttar Pradesh are as of now going through the stage where even if the political and economic powers do not exactly converge on the same set of caste groups, still there is mutual co-operation and support between them and they are as yet strong enough to resist change to the extent possible. If and when they have given in, more often than not it has been in response to the pressures mounted from below which occasionally have also been accompanied by violence.

Gujarat appears to be at a higher stage of evolutionary politics than the one in which the States of Bihar and Uttar Pradesh happen to be. The qualitative difference in the prevailing situation in Gujarat is that since 1980 onwards there has been a distinct polarisation of the castes who wield economic, and those who wield political power. The emergence of the group popularly known as KHAM consisting of the Kshatriyas, Harijans, Adivasis and the Muslims as a strong political force has for once put the dominant castes composed of the Patels, Vanias, Rajputs in certain areas, and the Brahmins largely out of the actual control of political power. The latter group however continues to have dominance in economic power. Actually the antireservation agitations of 1981 and 1985 are symptomatic of the frustrations and anger of the dominant castes who until 1980 had been in control of both economic and political power. Having been denied the political power that they had been used to wield, they apparently have begun to feel that the reservation of seats for technical education and for jobs would further erode the scarce opportunities open to the youths of their castes. This conflict between the castes, which is largely a product of the socio-economic change that is coming over Gujarat is at a critical stage. The anti-reservationist may have won an important battle. It cannot however be said that they have won the war. The issue continues to be open. Whether or not this polarisation will settle down to their respective areas of influence in the State as a whole remains to be seen. But this process of polarisation is an important stage in the evolution of politics and political power in the country.

One important point that needs to be noted is that those of the backward castes who are making good politically cannot be said to belong to the economically weaker sections in that group. There is the danger of this new class developing in due course, a vested interest which may set in motion a pattern similar to the earlier state of affairs except for the fact that the new incumbents themselves happen to be those drawn from what is referred to as OBCs, Scheduled Castes and Scheduled Tribes. In the process they may also try and exploit the weaker sections among them as is happening in some of the States. In the meantime, one expects that the vast mass of the weaker sections would acquire a higher degree of education and awareness and would be agitating to have their legitimate share in political power. This should lead to a further diffusion of political and economic power over larger segments of population.

Karnataka provides yet another stage which may even be cited as a level higher than that at which Gujarat stands today. In Karnataka, both the political and economic power have got diffused over the different groups which include the so-called upper as much as the lower castes. The Vokkaligas who had all along wielded considerable economic power and also political power were classified as a Backward Caste by Devraj Urs, in a shrewed move to enlist their support in the political game that he so skilfully and successfully played. Devraj Urs will be long remembered by the people of Karnataka as one who put politics to the best and proper use of being an agent of socio-economic change. Though some of the infirmities and iniquities of the caste system still persist in Karnataka, it is at a stage where it cannot be said to produce the type of violence and harassment that is suffered by the weaker sections in Bihar. Into this refreshingly appealing state of affairs has been introduced an incongruous political note in the wake of the Venkataswamy Commission report. The Karnataka Government has sought to mollify the agitated lower and the upper caste groups, who stood to lose the benefit of reservations, if the Venkataswamy Commission report was implemented, by totally rejecting its report. This only reinforces the conclusion that the concept of reservation which was intended as a restricted and self-limiting means to achieve the very desirable end of dissolving the centuries old caste system is tending to acquire unforseen potential for perpetuating the division of Indian society into so many different caste groups. What is worse, going by the anxiety of the several caste groups, not to part with reservation even though they are doing well socially and educationally, backwardness whether real or imagined has, during the last about four decades or so, been lifted from a stigma to the prestige of a desirable status.

Thus Bihar and Uttar Pradesh on the one side, Gujarat on the other and Karnataka as the third stream, constitute three different stages in the evolution of the socio-economic changes that have come about in the country since Independence. The conclusion that emerges from the foregoing is that the vested interests do not part with power even if resistance entails violence. It is only as and when the vested interests dissolve, that state power and the use of it become instruments for providing community well-being, and a healthy system of governance. Only in a system that provides for the political and economic participation of the greatest number, is there likely to be the least violence.

There is yet another aspect to violence. This depends on who employs it and in what context. Words such as violence, force, protest, and legitimacy as distinct from legality are all relative terms, depending for their exact relevance on the context in which they have been used. There is a large component of subjectivity in all their uses. The only manner in which this subjectivity can be converted into objective terms is to apply the test of means and ends. If we are honest enough to examine the context in which violence has been used, where, by whom and for what purpose, we will be able to avoid the fallacies and understand the phenomenon of violence in its proper perspective. Thus considered, violence may have a positive role, if in the existing scheme of things there are built-in distortions, disabilities and deprivations. If the system itself does not provde for the automatic removal of these, violence for removing the disequilibrium becomes the inescapable last resort. Thus considered, while violence per se may be undesirable, it has also to be viewed in the context in which this has been occuring.

The gap between the promises made at the Government level and the actual performance at the low level of the implementation have to be brought down to the irreducible minimum, if for whatever valid and practical reason, the gap cannot be eliminated completely. Hopes inspired in the minds of the socially and economically disadvantaged and deprived sections of the population through legislations will have to be fulfilled to the farthest extent possible.

In a plural society law's legitimate function is to help preserve harmony between different groups without giving the impression to any of the groups that it is enforced in a partial or partisan manner. The weaker and the deprived groups should not be driven to resort to violence out of a sense of frustration with the efficacy of law as an agent of change. Those in authority who will not enforce the rule of law uniformly but only selectively are jeopardising the freedom of every citizen. When law assumes different connotations to different individuals depending upon their socio-economic and political position the rule of law ceases to exist. Such distortions cannot go on without nature exacting a very high price somewhere along the way.

A very disturbing trend emerges out of this study. This has to do with the repeated instances of reluctance to imlement, if not the actual repudiation of the decisions validly arrived at responsible levels of Government. The circumstances in which the resolution passed by the Maharashtra State Council approving change of the name of the Marathwada University in to Ambedkar University is a case in point. The decision of the Gujarat Government not to implement the increased quota of reservation is yet another, though its relevance is merely theoretical as of now. Failure to implement categorically the decisions on the minimum wages by the several State Governments is yet another. The lukerwarmness with which the law abolishing the Bonded Labour system is implemented adds further to the list. The supreme example is the implementation of the Land Ceiling Laws and certain other aspects of Land Reforms which could be justifiably considered as blatant acts of evasion. In all these cases, the reasons that have prevailed with the Government have been the pressures of the vested interest silently applied, or violently registered with the co-operation of the officials in charge of implementation. Quite often those in charge of executive power have identified themselves with the vested interests. Such instances add up to one inescapable inference, and that is that violence in the ultimate analysis is an instrument of the stronger of the contending parties, groups or individuals. If the stronger of the parties represents the vested interests, they triumph with the help of actual or potential violence. If, however, the stronger party in terms of the volume of violence at its command is the mass of the people from below, they triumph over the rest. This drives us inexorably to the sad conclusion: violence when employed in adequate volume and intensity, often emerges as the arbiter of human destinies. This is where the State power has to come in assertively and decisively through the honest intervention of its institutions and agencies.

This study irresistably points to the conculsion that if the social change that is being sought to be attempted at different levels and in different fields is not accompained by appropriate and matching instituional "midwifery", the chances are that violence will take the place of institutions as it is already tending to do in some States. Violence at any rate in Bihar is tending to get raised to the level of a form of communication, a kind of language. One gets the impression that those who resort to this form of communication have arrived at this stage probably because they have not been able to make themselves heard through the normally accepted medium and instituions of communication. That the Government has spent vast sums on the administrative structure is not the same thing as producing the capability for handling the fall-out from the several problems which are concomitants of social change. Social change has certainly made violence possible but not inevitable. It becomes inevitable only to the extent of inadequacy and ineffectivencess of the institutional infrastructure in general and in particular of the Criminal Justice System. Ineffectiveness of a system can be due either to: (1) infirmities inherent in the institutions because of their inappropriateness for handling the types of situations generated by social change or (2) the subversion of the institutions by their operators through partisanship, corruption or even indifference. Our institutions can be faulted on both these counts. Our democracy is just about four decades old. If during these early but vital years, there has been failure to build into the institutions a degree of vitality and purity, even the most robust and efficient of institutions are bound to be corroded and their effectiveness blunted. Violence easily and inevitably moves into such a situation with results which will be painful for all. We have to face the fact that corruption in its different connotations has taken a very heavy toll of the vitality and effectiveness of our administrative and other institutions and this has, in no small measure contributed to the prevailing violence in some of the States. Capability of an institution by itself is not self-executing. It requires a degree of commitment on the part of its functionaries, which is what in the ultimate analysis determines the nature and quality of the performance of institutions. That institutional arrangement is the best which bridges the gap between capability and commitment. This is turn will automatically take care of the gap between what is possible and what is desirable.

If the conflicting forces are to be prevented from establishing their respective interests through violence, the State in a democratic set up has to step in as a credible agent capable of resolving the conflicting interests of the contending groups according to accepted, and predetermined norms. The state has to exercise its power in favour of or against contending factions, if it is to fulfil its fundamental role as an agent of change. It is the capability and performance of the Government, and not merely the stated intentions that impress. Mere promises are not enough. The political functionaries have to fulfil their obligation as elected representatives. It means the availability of an actively functioning and healthy political forum and/or voluntary organisations like the Trade Unions as a permanent and integral part of the institutions facilitating the process of change. In the absence of an appropriate forum capable of channelling the grievances of the people into a programmed plan of action, the discontent among the people degenerates into anger and frustrations. This in turn creates conditions for social despair and aggressive assertion of rights, as in the case of minimum wages or tenurial rights. The unresolved economic disabilities snowball into widespread and indiscriminate violence. This absence of a suitable forum is a common denominator that characterises the set-up in most of the States. To seek social change without providing for the fall out from it is not to understand the fundamentals of social engineering.

If politicians and political parties do not employ politics as an agent of change according to certain accepted and basic ground rules governing the actions of the political functionaries up and down a well-defined and visible hierarchical line, violence will take the place of political adhocism which will then masquerade as a legitimate political process This is what is happening in some of the States. A sensitive and disciplined political party with an ideological base is normally expected to channel causes capable of contributing to violence at their incipient stage. The absence of such political parties functioning on a day-to-day basis with comprehensive contacts with the different and conflicting elements which should be an integral part of public life at all levels, is a phenomenon common to a number of States, and particularly to some of those ruled by the Congress party. In States like Bihar, and to an extent Uttar Pradesh, what the party in power largely depends on are the local heavy weights, who may be landowners, contractors or families traditionally enjoying local loyalties, who are coopted by the party in power for mobilising political support in times of political instability, and particularly during elections. Such an adhoc arrangement is hardly sensitive to public grievances and is certainly not intended to project to the political powers that be the problems at the grass root levels with a view to get them sorted out administratively. The Congress party as it is functioning in some of the States, gives the impression of a tenuous coalition of conflicting interests incapable of pursuing its own legislations to their logical end for fear of antagonising the dominant vested interests among the coalition partners. This is in sharp contrast to the situation obtaining in West Bengal since, 1977. Caste and class domination has been weakened in West Bengal, and this has had its beneficial impact on the nature and the quantum of violence in that State. The violence in that State as of now is largely a product of inter-political conflicts. Atul Kohli's paper characterises the CPM leadership as a shared but cohesive group. "The CPM leadership views political survival as an on going struggle with 'reactionary forces'. Party discipline and the perception of continuing struggle have thus facilitated cohesive rule and coherent policies in contemporary West Bengal...... The CPM seeks to preserve democratic institutions while using State power to facilitate development with redistribution"[2]. The key linkage groups have been the students with rural roots who come to the city for education, get politicised and go back to rural areas to teach and to serve as party organizers and propagaters. As these students often come from the middle-income families, the social base of the CPM in both the cities and the countryside rests on the middle class strata. The party also gets its support from the widespread lower income groups. Several interested groups contribute to this. They are the movements of the students, teachers, trade unions, the peasants and the landless labour. These different groups constitute the link between the party and the society at large. Electoral and political support is mobilised through these different organisations. The difference in the functioning of a party like the CPM in West Bengal in their dealings with the day-to-day problems of the people is in such sharp contrast to the functioning of the Congress in some other States. The absence of strong caste identities in Bengal compared to Bihar and Uttar Pradesh explains why the upper caste Hindus have been able to forge political links with the lower caste peasants and workers. Diluted caste identities in West Bengal should also enable us to understand "the failure of Bengal's non-communist parties in mobilising along dominant caste lines or in utilising high caste influentials as vote banks[3]

One point that needs highlighting with regard to the conversion of the Harijans of Meenakshipuram to Islam is that these Harijans were far more advanced educationally and materially than the general run of the Harijans in certain other parts of the country. Among the 1250 Harijans there were two MBBS doctors and agricultural scientists and five graduates. A number of them held government jobs and two of the four teachers of local primary schools were Harijans. Out of 180 families, 80 families owned land and the largest land holder was a Harijan with about 10 acres of land. Those who did not have land or those who had marginal holdings were cultivators of the Temple estate. What eventually drove the Harijans to convert thmselves to Islam was not so much their economic condition, as the continued social discrimination and disabilities that they were subjected to by the Thevars, an intermediate caste group. This phenomenon is extremely relevant in the context of the upward social mobility of the Harijans. While even the economic deprivation which is bad in itself may continue to be put up with upto a point, people will no longer tolerate, much less accept the social discrimination that has been a feature of this country's traditional social hierarchical set up.

Unless there is an attitudinal change of the caste groups towards those who, until Independence, had been assigned to the bottom of the social ladder, the country is in for violent social upheaval and convulsion, the nature and extent of which it is difficult to forecast. The reaction of the Meenakshipuram Harijans and the realignment of political forces in Gujarat through what has come to be termed as KHAM, are straws in the wind which will have far reaching social and political impact. These aspects bring out in emphatic terms that the caste factor in the Indian social political scene, if continued socially and exploited politically, will lead to a realignment of the Indian society in terms and patterns as never known before.

The Indian society in its present state of transition, is like a chrysalis in metamorphosis. The chrysalis may evolve and become a butterfly or die, but it clearly cannot prevert to the caterpillar stage. Is the Indian society prepared to recognise and adjust itself to the fact that what it is called upon to confront is not just surface disturbance, but a groundswell which calls into question certain traditionally accepted valucs of life? Adapt or perish has been the ruthless law of nature for all its children. Are we prepared?

According to one estimate, even in 2000 A.D. 70% of India's population is likely to be rural-based. This means that there will be considerable tension, and even violence, if adequate steps are not taken to forestall and counter them. Elections to the Parliament, Assembiles, Jilla Parishads and the Panchayats have introduced considerable potential for violence in the rural areas, not only at the time of the elections but also long afterwards, depending on the trail of bitterness that all elections keenly contested leave behind. Population growth in the rural areas will add to the increase in the number of landless agricultural labourers. Peasant agitations organized by the landless will aggravate and unsettle conditions arising out of the scarcity of resources. Except in the case of Gujarat where the caste conflicts surfaced in a very pronounced form in some urban centres during the 1980 and 1985 agitations, this phenomenon is largely a feature of the rural areas in the other states. Even during the Marathwada agitation which had its origin on an issue which was primarily urban, much of the violence took place in the distant villages, though certain urban centres were also not free from it. It is therefore imperative that the Criminal Justice System which is primarily urban-oriented is suitably spread locationally, if it is to fulfil its legitimate role correctly and promptly. This has special relevance to the judiciary and the police. The policing of the country today is primarily urban-oriented Not enought thinking or study has gone into the nature and the type of problems that we will be called upon to face in the rural areas. In this connection, the insufficiency of the rural Police Stations both in terms of their numerical strength and their locations which are not strategic enough, inadequacy of the infrastructural back up in terms of roads, transport and communication are factors which contribute to making the policing of the rural areas increasingly difficult in the face of the mounting challenges. If the several sources of tension are not attended to adequately, appropriately and in time by organized institutional effort from above, violence from below from these several centres will become inevitable. To bring out a significant segment of the Indian population out of a feudalistic past into an egalitarian present is not going to be easy, nor is it likely to be free from violence. The measure of the statemanship of our leaders and the institutional capability and commitment, will be judged by the level to which violence is kept down in the process of transforming our society on the lines of the Constitutional goal that we have set ourselves.

It is not always that the 'order' imposed by the police is in consonance with the 'law', though the two terms which have come to be wedded, go together. It is time that the authorities realised that in dealing with the dacoits and the Naxalites often the 'order' achieved at such high human costs is brutally at variance with the imperatives of the 'law'; or is it that they have realised the factual position and it suits them to go along quietly with the Police, to get along conveniently with the system? An administration which is indifferent in its reactions to the fake encounters with dacoits or the so-called Naxalites can and will over a period of time come to believe in the genuineness of the claims that its functionaries are making on its behalf. This, in turn, will result in a growing disinclination on the part of the Government to subject these claims to any serious internal scrutiny. Such indifference can generate a type of work ethics among the administrative and law enforcing agencies, from the damaging consequences of which even the most law abiding citizens will not be able to escape. Accountability for the responsible use of power by its wielders is a must even in the best of times. In the seething social brew such as the one that we are living through, this accountability is a categorical imperative.

The violence that has rocked some of our cities and towns in the vecent past has a special message which we can ignore only at our peril. The economically deprived and the socially backward will no longer wait for a happy and peaceful transition from their present deprived status to a higher level of economic and social mobility. With the social and political awareness that they have developed, the message to live on more and better consumer goods displayed in the catchy advertisements in the television hour after hour, day after day, are not lost on this class of the deprived sections of the population. They as a class are in a hurry to make good the lost time. Their children demand more and better amenities and they see no reason why they should be denied items of goods which a neighbour or even someone further away has. It needs to be mentioned that there is widespread hostility and bitterness among the millions who have not shared the nation's limited prosperity. There is visible anger and yet a sullen acceptance of the conditions for the time being. The threshold of tolerance is likely to shrink fast. No democratic government can long endure without serious damage to its structure and stability, with the existance, within its major urban centres and the rural areas of millions of citizens below the poverty line, who as a group understandably feel deeply aggrieved.

If the socio-economic change that is being held out by the leaders is not ushered in as a perceptible programme of every day life, the change may well force itself violently at irreparable cost to society. Evidently, the vast mass of people still nurse the hope that the Government would be able to bring about the much needed change in the foreseable future. One cannot dare predict how long this will hold in an atmosphere of rootlessness of mobile people; loosening of the traditional social organisations and decline of the influence of religion as legitimsing the inherited social system and inducing a degree of fatalistic acceptance of things as they are. The picture is not being overdrawn. The intention is merely to emphasise the message to those who ought to listen. This will call for a resolute and determined effort at norm setting. It is most unrealistic to ask for a society without violence if there is politicisation of criminals, or criminalisation of politics, and an unholy alliance between those in power, in administration and in business leading to deals which are contributing in no small measure to the generation of black money, corruption and a parallel black economy

Above all, we would do well to abandon our faith in a police solution to problems which are born essentially of unresolved and evaded socio-economic issues. The police cannot be expected to take the responsibility of sorting out the results of wrong political and economic decisions taken by the government. To do so would be to give a role to the police which it cannot and should not have in a democratic system.

According to the paper prepared by the Planning Commission on the Seventh Five Year Plan the addition to the labour force in the next fifteen years will be about 120 million persons. Taking into account the estimated backlog of unemployment as of 1985 the over all magnitude of additional employment to be generated by the year 2000 would be around 130 million. But the figures as registered by the Employment Exchanges all over the country as on 31-12-1985 stood at 26 million which is vastly different from the Planning Commission's figures of 9.2 million. But even going by the figures of the Planning Commission, the situation would constitute a major challenge which will have to be met by the creation of additional employment opportunities. Since there will always be a segment of people left out of employment, this can be a source of violence. This can get further compounded if among those thus left out there are significant segments of population belonging to the minorities and the weaker sections. It will therefore have to be ensured that not only is there adequate employment opportunities but that these get distributed fairly between the different segments of the employment seekers. Failure to do so will have the potentials of communal and caste violence.

The demographic perspective also implies a progressive decline in the size of land holdings. The problems consequent on this will have to be met by removing the obstacles to increased productivity of small farms, which will entail significant institutional improvement in the delivery system of the various extension services which are intimately connected with agriculture. The whole process will have to be institutionalised in a manner that the vested interests among the landholders are not able to thwart the upward social mobility of the weaker sections by colluding with the functionaries manning the administrative and developmental infrastructure.

According to the Planning Commission, the population in the year 2,000 is estimated to reach 972 million. This projection has been made apparently on the assumption that the Family Welfare Programme will be implemented effectively and uniformly. The growth of population would, by itself increase the areas of tension by the mere fact of the limited resources having to go around an ever-expanding population. But this problem is likely to get further accentuated if the family welfare programme leads to differential growth of population between the communities. This trend is already evident in some of the states. Considering the potentials that unequal growth in population holds, which in turn will impinge on several other factors such as education, employment and other opportunities, it would be worth our while to ensure that the Family Wellfare Programme is accepted uniformly by all the communities.

The urban population in the year 2.000 A.D. is expected to be nearly 315 million indicating a share of 32% of the total population. This is roughly 54% of the total addition to population between 1981 and the year 2.000 A.D Unless there is a corresponding increase and improvement at the level and quality of the urban housing and civic amenities, the problems created by the shortfall can generate considerable urban tension. It is expected that by 2000 A.D., 60% of the villages would be connected by all weather roads as against the present 34%. That being so, the urban tensions generally, and particularly of the communal variety, can travel from the urban to the rural hinterland much faster and with greater damage to life and property.

Inspite of planning over the years, the plan projections have not always been fulfilled in certain sectors of particular importance to social well being and harmony. The comulative shortfalls in the matter of employment, education, housing and the basic civic amenities can contribute to the creation of deep discontent because of frustrated hopes and unfulfilled aspirations of the millions, which can erupt into mindless violence. Only timely and effective action of the authorities concerned at the Centre and in the states, can prevent this frightening prospect from becoming a reality.

The study of the various incidents reported from different parts of the country indicates that there is no single theory of conflict resolution which can be applied uniformly to all the conflict situations in different parts of the country. There are a variety of causes and even the same causes do not have an identical outcome every where.
As we survey the scene in some of the states, it is apparent that Indian society is in a state of flux, even if the general framework has not changed significantly. There are very distinct and discernible signs of changes that are coming over in society, with a still largely unaltered social structure.

There is no rigid and uniform alignment of forces in terms of class, caste or groups. The alignment varies from state to state, and even within a state, depending upon the nature of the issues involved and their relevance in the local socio-economic context. Since the benefits accruing from reservations have to be availed of, and the reservations are based on caste, there is no likelihood of caste as an identity disappearing in the near future, though its implications in practice may get increasingly diluted in the urban and semi-urban centres.

As Sardar Patel had observed years ago: "It will be folly to ignore realities; facts take their revenge if they are not faced squarely". (5) It is time that the realities arising out of the socio-economic changes of the last two decades are faced in all their grim implications.

The choice is open. The direction of change is unmistakable. Do we have the necessary political and administrative will and wisdom to give the people of this country at least peace amidst the several disabilities inherent in an economy under strain because of an exploding population and scarcity of resources and opportunities?

We as a nation are capable of doing much better than what we are doing at present in terms of administrative competence and giving a fair and honest deal to our entire population. That we are hamstrung by the traditions of caste, feudalism and colonial inheritance need not make us underestimate our capability for rising above each and every one of the legacies from our past. What is necessary above all, is to recover our faith in ourselves and work to build up a better and a cleaner society in which those who ask for payment of minimum wages, and certainty of tenurial rights on lands cultivated by them, need not be shot down by labelling them as Naxalities, where the majority is without tyranny and the minorities without fear, where the Government does the proper thing not only when it is expedient to do so, but because it is right, and all our people can count on a happy future.

Reference:

1. Andre Beteille : "Equality as a right and as a policy" (1986)
2. Atul Kohli's paper : From elite Radicalism to Democrate Consolidation : The rise of Reform Communism in West Bengal (1984).
3. IBID—Atul Kohli's paper
4. Nikhil Lakshman : "Despair, Frustration and Anger", Illustrated Weekly of India, 30th November, 1986.
5. Sri L.P. Singh : "Sardar Patel and the Indian Administration." Sardar Patel Memorial Lecture, Surat, 15th December, 1986.

Annexures

Annexure A

NUMBER OF AGRICULTURAL LABOURERS IN INDIA STATE-WISE

State/Union Territory	Number of Agricultural Labourers			
	1951	1961	1971	1981
Andhra Pradesh		5336494	6828685	8325017
Assam		187416	405998	—
Bihar		4418475	6806103	7366973
Gujarat		1252000	1887660	2488300
Haryana		—	430312	590324
Himachal Pradesh		11332	53344	40072
Jammu & Kashmir		18417	41933	63540
Karnataka		1761110	2717537	3655197
Kerala		978396	1908114	1917362
Madhya Pradesh		2815200	4062338	4857829
Maharashtra		4510002	5393138	6470855
Manipur		2184	13525	28613
Meghalaya		—	44131	57899
Nagaland		2501	3797	2979
Orissa		1303511	1937574	2396974
Punjab		543795	786705	1092225
Rajasthan		393631	749116	764625
Sikkim		2230	4207	4887

Tamil Nadu	2828374	4490065	6037601
Tripura	32912	86340	146089
Uttar Pradesh	3261178	5453829	5177074
West Bengal	1771708	3272198	3891531
TRRITORIES			
Andaman & Nicobar Island	348	2137	2337
Arunachal Pradesh	—	5292	7796
Chandigarh	—	1266	856
Dadra & Nagar Haveli	4949	5934	4592
Delhi	7325	15269	16131
Goa, Daman & Diu	39336	40768	32394
Lakshadweep	—	—	—
Mizoram	10	—	5118
Pondicherry	38807	46275	54514
All-India TOTAL	31521641	47493590	55499704

Source : Census Data

Annexure B

SCHEDULED CASTES & SCHEDULED TRIBES
NUMBER OF AGRICULTURAL LABOURERS IN INDIA STATE-WISE

S.No.	State/Union Territory	SC/ ST	Number of Agricultural Labourers 1951	1961	1971	1981
1.	Andhra Pradesh	SC		1756908	2126833	2734910
		ST		276409	383595	685778
2.	Assam	SC		12986	34712	—
		ST		32768	29141	—
3.	Bihar	SC		1761377	2380867	2692623
		ST		236458	481950	500606
4.	Gujarat	SC		168235	280355	315761
		ST		460121	637842	788506
5.	Haryana	SC		—	261211	365085
		ST		—	—	—
6.	Himachal Pradesh	SC		6794	28446	18496
		ST		702	2149	2077
7.	Jammu & Kashmir	SC		3272	9764	14097
		ST		—	—	—

S.No.	State/Union Territory	SC/ ST	1951	Number of Agricultural 1961	Labourers 1971	1981
30.	Mizoram	SC		—	—	—
		ST		—	491	4314
31.	Pondicherry	SC		19647	23953	20388
		ST		—	—	—
32.	All-India TOTAL	SC		10453759	15044761	18249360
		ST		3334455	4832427	7174898

Source : Census Data

DISTRIBUTION

Communities	Year	Total Main Workers	Cultivators
A.P.	1971	180373399	78176707
		(100.0)	(43.4)
	1981	222516574	92522835
		(100.0)	(41.6)
S.C.	1971	29071359	8101567
		(100.0)	(27.9)
	1981	37844568	10661128
		(100.0)	(28.2)
S.T.	1971	14624441	8418491
		(100.0)	(57.6)
	1981	21963688	11954765
		(100.0)	(54.4)

Source: Census 1971 and 1981

Figures in brackets are the percentages to the total Main Workers

A.P. = All Persons

S.C. = Scheduled Castes

S.T. = Scheduled Tribes

Annexure C

OF WORKERS

Agricultural Labourers	Household Industries Manufacturing, processing, Repairs	Others
47489383	6351714	48354589
(26.3)	(3.5)	(26.8)
55499704	7710920	66783115
(24.9)	(3.5)	(30.0)
15044761	967225	4957806
(51.8)	(3.3)	(17.0)
18249360	1252502	7681578
(48.2)	(3.3)	(20.3)
4832427	150486	1223037
(33.0)	(1.0)	(8.4)
7174898	311865	2522160
(32.7)	(1.4)	(11.5)

Annexure CI

PERCENTAGE OF LAND ALLOTTED TO SCHEDULED CASTES AND SCHEDULED TRIBES

1

S.No.	State/UT	Percentage of SC to total No. of agricultural labourers (1981)	Percentage of land allotted to SC	Percentage of ST to total No. of Agricultural labourers (1981)	Percentage of land allotted to ST
1	2	3	4	5	6
1.	Andhra Pradesh	32.98	45.18	8.27	17.75
2.	Assam (1971)	*	6.89	*	9.93
3.	Bihar	36.68	53.00	6.82	13.00
4.	Gujarat	12.58	76.78	31.40	11.71
5.	Haryana	62.04	47.43	(No ST)	—
6.	Himachal Pradesh	44.01	69.56	4.94	4.00
7.	Karnataka	29.23	54.19	8.80	2.24
8.	Kerala	28.25	36.18	3.20	7.83
9.	Madhya Pradesh	23.77	24.99	35.95	47.90
10.	Maharashtra	12.98	32.78	19.22	18.14
11.	Manipur	0.82	Nil	8.72	Nil

12. Orissa	27.94	31.09	35.73	42.93
13. Punjab	71.13	49.15	(No ST)	—
14. Rajasthan	41.86	34.52	17.41	12.65
15. Tamil Nadu	43.13	32.58	1.43	0.02
16. Tripura	18.63	22.01	41.83	18.78
17. Uttar Pradesh	49.25	59.23	0.12	N.A.
18. West Bengal	39.32	41.10	16.13	19.50
19. Dadra & Nagar Haveli		0.77	0.82	96.30
99.12				
20. Delhi	42.92	N.A.	(No ST)	—
21. Pondichery	51.79	66.67	(No ST)	—
Total	33.00		12.88	
India	32.96	36.95	12.96	14.57

* Census could not be held in Assam owing to disturbed conditions prevailing there at the time of 1981 Census. The 1971 Census of Assam which included Mizoram at that time returned the total number of agricultural labourers as 4,05,998 and that of SC and ST as 34,712 (8.55%) and 29,632 (7.30%) respectively.

C1 and C2, From the Vth Report of the Commission on SCs. and S.Ts.

Statement showing the progress of allotment of ceiling surplus land to

Sl. No.	State/Union Territory	Areas estimated to be surplus	Area declared surplus	Area taken possession of	Total Area distri-buted
1	2	3	4	5	6
1.	Andhra Pradesh	10,09,323@	10,09,323	4,42,766	3,17,583
2.	Assam	5,68,873@	5,68,873	4,89,675	3,22,015
3.	Bihar	3,00,000	2,48,192	1,52,249	1,49,360
4.	Gujarat	1,63,572	1,63,572	69,846	12,045
5.	Haryana	30,380	29,228	20,437	20,173
6.	Himachal Pradesh	3,35,881	1,13,971	1,12,635	3,344
7.	Karnataka	4,00,000	2,95,720	1,48,039	1,04,920
8.	Kerala	1,50,000	1,24,604	81,782	54,422
9.	Madhya Pradesh	2,56,484@	2,56,484	1,45,788	87,884
10.	Maharashtra	3,70,658	3,70,193	2,81,586	2,81,586
11.	Manipur	1,819	1,029	159	37
12.	Orissa	2,00,000	1,47.775	1,23,798	1,06,992
13.	Punjab	46,682@	46,682	17,014	13,353
14.	Rajasthan	7,94,000	2,60,533	2,32,517	1,32,185
15.	Tamil Nadu	2,04,395	87,951	81,267	63,654
16.	Tripura	5,187	1,690	1,558	1,113
17.	Uttar Pradesh	2,88,081	2,88,081	2,64,167	2,36,675
18.	West Bengal	1,72,467	1,64,767	1,12,818	62,460
19.	Dadra & Nagar Haveli	9,390	8,958	6,776	3,616
20.	Delhi	1,500	722	374	374(b)
21.	Pondicherry	3,210	2,560	1,132	927
	Total	53,11,902	41,90,908	27,86,383	19,74,718

@ These figures have been revised/readjusted upwards to tally with the area already declared surplus as the figures of area estimated surplus given by the State Government are lower than those of area already reported as declared surplus.

(b) The Agrarian Reforms Act 1976, was enacted and brought into fore only recently and no report on the progress made has yet been received.

(c) Extent of area has been estimated in proportion to the number of beneficiaries since the State Govt. has furnished only the break-up of total number of beneficiaries and not of total area distributed.

(d) Includes Scheduled Tribes also.

(e) Includes an area of 88052 acres given to 64881 beneficiaries belonging to other backward classes.

(f) Includes an area of 13641 acres given to institutions.

ANNEXURE C2

the Scheduled Castes, Scheduled Tribes and others for the period upto 4th March 1983)

(In acres)

Total No. of beneficiaries	Scheduled Castes		Scheduled Tribes		Others	
	Area distributed	No. of beneficiaries	Area distributed	No. of beneficiaries	Area distributed	No. of beneficiaries
7	8	9	10	11	12	13
2,27,152	1,43,472	1,11,171	56,386	36,862	1,17,725 (e)	79,119
2,75,617	22,175	22,544	31,990	20,617	2,67,850 (f)	2,32,456
1,68,690	79,161 (c)	94,864	19,417(c)	17,741	50,782(c)	56,085
2,900	9,248	2,158	1,410	364	1,387	378
5,830	9,568	2,807	—	—	10,605	3,023
4,362	2,326	2,906	134	262	884	1,194
24,383	56,854	14,292	2,349	613	45,717	9,478
89,588	19,693	36,448	4,261	5,247	30,468(g)	47,893
34,455	21,965	9,944	42,096	14,255	23,823	10,256
76,892	92,294	24,418	51,072	15,675	1,38,220	36,799
18	—	—	—	—	37	18
82,180	33,266	27,655	45,902	32,072	27,824	22,453
3,141	6,563	1,476	—	—	6,790	1,665
29,040	45,634	11,676	16,718	4,247	69,833(h)	13,117
43,219	20,739	19,846	12	15	42,903	23,358
1,002	245	274	209	150	659	578
1,93,926	1,40,189	1,43,726(d)	—	—	96,486	50,200
1,76,461	25,671(c)	72,454	12,180(c)	34,333	24,609(c)	69,583
1,613	30	13	3,584	1,599	2	1
—	—	—	—	—	374(i)	—
1,036	618	749	—	—	309	287
14,41,505	7,29,711	5,99,512	2,87,720	1,84,052	9,57,287	6,57,951

(g) Includes an area of 3006 acres given to 3 institutions.

(h) Includes an area of 3882 acres handed over to the Tamil Nadu Sugar Cane Farm Corporation Limited and 8456 acres reserved under Disposal of Surplus Land Rules, 1966.

(i) Area distributed to institutions/societies.

Important Cases of

Name of place of occurance	Date of Crime	Date of Judgement	No. of persons killed/injured: Caste Hindu M K	Caste Hindu M I	Caste Hindu F K	Caste Hindu F I	Caste Hindu C K	Caste Hindu C I	Harijans M K	Harijans M I	Harijans F K	Harijans F I	Harijans C K	Harijans C I	other damages
BELCHI (Bihar)	27-5-77	19-5-80	3	-	-	-	-	-	8	-	-	-	-	-	—
PIPRA (Bihar)	25-2-80	5-8-81	-	-	-	-	-	-	7	2	6	-	1	-	26 huts burnt
KAILA (Bihar)	9-12-78	7-10-80	-	-	-	-	-	-	3	14	-	-	-	-	Out of three dead two beheaded
BISHRAMPUR (Bihar)	25-3-78	11-4-81	-	-	-	-	-	-	3	34	-	-	-	-	18 houses burnt
KAFALTA (U.P.)	9-5-80	15-4-81	1	4	-	-	-	-	14	4	-	-	-	-	1 hut burnt
JETALPUR (Gujarat)	26-12-80	31-8-81	-	-	-	-	-	-	1	-	-	-	-	-	—
PALPUR (U.P.)	13-2-81	20-6-82	-	-	-	-	-	-	3	14	-	-	-	-	
SOHWALIA (Bihar)	7-6-81	24-7-84													—
DHARAMPURA (Bihar)	20-10-77	8-7-84	-	-	-	-	-	-	4	6	-	-	-	-	—
DEOLI (U.P.)	19-11-81		-	-	-	-	-	-	9	7	6	-	9	-	—
SADOPUR	30-12-81		-	-	-	-	-	-	2	2	5	3	3	-	—

Source: Scheduled Castes Backward Classes Division, M.H.A.

Note: M-Male
F-Female
C-Child
K-Killed
I-Injured

Annexure D

Atrocities on Harijans

Cause of crime	Result of Judgements				Remarks
	Death sentence	Life Imprisenment	Other Punishments	Acquitted	
	2	15	—	7	—
No definite cause	—	50	—	11	1 Person dead
Land dispute	—	3	8 (2 yrs.)	3	—
Revenge and Animosity	—	27	—	4	—
Prevalent custom that Harijan bridegroom should not be carried in a Doli through the village	—	—	—	33	State Govt. has filed an appeal in High Court.
1) Money dealing between Rajputs and Patel. 2) Theft by the deceased	—	3	—	7	—
Non-Payment of wages	-	38	—	12	—
	4	20	—	—	—
Land dispute (Bataidari)	—	48	—	—	—
Enmity	—	—	—	—	—

Cases Registered Under PCR Act 1955 and their

Year	Disposal by Police				
	Brought Forward	No. of fresh cases Regd.	Total	Cases Challaned a in court	Brought Forward
1977	226	3425	3651	2920	2273
1978	247	4729	4976	3751	3953
1979	396	4911	5307	3444	4803
1980	927	4303	5230	3550	5579
1981	698	4085	4783	2865	4995
1982	690	4087	4777	2665	4547

Source : Ministry of Home Affairs (Annual Report on the PCR

Annexure E

Disposal by Police and Court

Disposal by Court			Results of cases in Court	
Fresh Challened cases in court	Total	Cases Disposed of by court	Convicted	Acquitted
2920	5193	2014	551 (27.36%)	1463 (72.64%)
3751	7704	2492	490 (19.66%)	2002 (80.34%)
3444	8247	2675	613 (22.92%)	2062 (77.08%)
3550	9129	4133	1267 (30.66%)	2866 (69.34%)
2865	7860	2526	441 (17.46%)	2085 (82.54%)
2665	7212	1832	199 (10.86%)	1633 (89.14%)

Act 1955 for the years 1981-82).

Statement regarding the cases registered under the Protection of

State/Union Territory	Brought forwarded with Police	Court	Number of cases registered fresh	Number of cases closed by police after investigation but without challaning
1	2	3	4	5
Andhra Pradesh	46	152	238	29
Assam	Nil	Nil	1	Nil
Bihar	25	107	17	2
Gujarat	28	555	281	25
Haryana	Nil	11	6	2
Jammu & Kashmir**	1	10	5	—
Himachal Pradesh	1	23	16	5
Karnataka	116	772	581	90
Kerala	5	49	38	24
Madhya Pradesh**	3	777	237	—
Maharashtra*	297	1,021	998	325
Orissa	15	312	106	37
Punjab	Nil	1	Nil	Nil
Rajasthan	8	221	173	67
Tamil Nadu	84	534	1136	277
Uttar Pradesh	58	431	224	91
Chandigarh	2	Nil	2	2
Delhi	8	13	10	3
Goa, Daman & Diu	Nil	Nil	2	Nil
Pondicherry	1	6	14	3
Total (1981)	698	4,995	4,085	982
Total (1980)	927	5,579	4,303	982
Increase or decrease over 1980	—229	—584	—218	Static
Percentage increase or decrease over 1980.	—24.70	—10.47	—5.07	Static

Note : * The latest figure of number of cases brought forwarded with court received from the Government of Maharashtra has been adopted.
** Correct figure of disposal of cases awaited from the Government of Jammu & Kashmir and Madhya Pradesh.
N/A Not available.
From Manipur, Meghalaya, Nagaland, Tripura, West Bengal & Nicobar Island, Arunachal Pradesh, Dadra & Nagar Haveli, Lakshadweep and Mizoram no case has been reported.

Annexure EI

Civil Rights Act, 1955 and their disposal during the year 1981

Number of cases challaned in the court	Number of cases disposed off by court			Number of cases pending at the end of the year with	
	ending in cnviction	ending aquittal	Total	Police	Court
6	7	8	9	10	11
132	7	54	61	123	223
1	Nil	Nil	Nil	Nil	1
12	N/A	6	6	28	113
263	18	436	454	21	364
3	1	9	10	1	4
—	—	—	—	—	—
12	3	14	17	Nil	18
455	79	313	392	152	835
18	Nil	25	25	1	42
—	—	—	—	—	—
801	191	568	759	169	1063
26	6	58	64	58	274
Nil	Nil	Nil	Nil	Nil	1
91	31	57	88	23	224
867	66	489	555	76	846
159	31	51	82	32	508
Nil	Nil	Nil	Nil	2	Nil
11	1	Nil	1	4	23
2	Nil	1	1	Nil	1
12	7	4	11	Nil	7
2,865	441	2085	2,526	690	4,547
3,550	1,267	2,866	4,133	698	4,996
—685	—826	—781	—1607	—8	—449
—19.30	—65.19	—27.25	—38.88	—1.15	—8.99

Statement regarding the cases registered under the Protection of

State/Union Territory	Brought forwarded with		Number of cases registered fresh	Number of cases closed by police after investigation but without challaning
	Police	Court		
1	2	3	4	5
Andhra Pradesh	123	223	263	50
Assam	Nil	1	Nil	Nil
Bihar	28	113	28	4
Gujarat	21	364	347	36
Haryana	1	4	5	5
Jammu & Kashmir**	—	—	4	—
Himachal Pradesh	Nil	18	6	1
Karnataka*	152	835	674	88
Kerala	1	42	29	8
Madhya Pradesh**	—	—	337	—
Maharashtra*	169	1,063	769	211
Orissa	58	274	125	60
Punjab	Nil	1	4	Nil
Rajasthan	23	224	186	86
Tamil Nadu	76	846	1,105	262
Uttar Pradesh	32	508	186	73
Delhi	4	23	3	3
Chandigarh	2	Nil	1	2
Goa, Daman & Diu	Nil	1	3	1
Pondicherry	Nil	7	12	4
Total (1982)	690	4,547	4,087	894
Total (1981)	698	4,996	4,085	982
Increase or decrease over 1981	−8	−449	+2	−88
Percentage increase or decrease over 1981.	−1.15	−8.99	+0.05	−8.96

Note : * Disposal of Brought forward cases awaited from the Government of Karnataka.

** Correct figures of Brought Forward cases and disposal of cases awaited from the Government of Jammu & Kashmir and Madhya Pradesh.

Annexure E2

Civil Rights Act, 1955 and their disposal during the year 1982

Number of cases challaned in the court	Number of cases disposed off by court			Number of cases pending at the end of the year with	
	ending in cnviction	ending in aquittal	Total	Police	Court
6	7	8	9	10	11
163	13	71	84	173	302
Nil	Nil	Nil	Nil	Nil	1
12	N/A	N/A	N/A	40	125
328	17	420	437	4	255
1	Nil	Nil	Nil	Nil	5
—	—	—	—	—	—
5	Nil	11	11	Nil	12
403	1	22	23	183	380
17	Nil	29	29	5	30
—	—	—	—	—	—
657	57	273	330	70	1390
75	10	57	67	48	282
4	Nil	3	3	Nil	2
108	24	34	58	15	274
755	51	594	645	164	956
126	23	104	127	19	507
2	1	1	2	2	23
Nil	Nil	Nil	Nil	1	Nil
1	Nil	1	1	1	1
8	2	13	15	Nil	Nil
2,665	199	1,633	1,832	725	4,545
2,865	441	2,085	2,526	690	4,547
—200	—242	—452	—694	+35	—2
—6.98	—54.88	—21.68	—27.47	+5.07	—0.04

N/A Not available.
From Manipur, Meghalaya, Nagaland, Tripura, West Bengal, Andaman & Nicobar Islands, Arunachal Pradesh, Dadra & Nagar Haveli, Lakshadeep, Mizoram no case has been reported.

Annexure E 3

COMPARATIVE STATEMENT SHOWING STATE-WISE BREAK-UP OF ATROCITY CASES COMMITTED ON SCHEDULED CASTES DURING 1979, 1980, 1981 and 1982

State/Union Territory	Number of cases reported during			
	1979	1980	1981	1982
1	2	3	4	5
Andhra Pradesh	92	152	206	213
Assam	03	Nil	Nil	Nil
Bihar	2,152	1,890	1,983	2,073
Gujarat	475	498	654	455
Himachal Pradesh	83	68	69	73
Haryana	80	78	74	144
Jammu & Kashmir	114	120	124	45
Karnataka	500	377	397	363
Madhya Pradesh	3,866	3,877	4,033	4,749
Kerala	887	478	260	145
Maharashtra	503	518	695	680
Orissa	43	80	80	150
Punjab	171	79	51	73
Rajasthan	760	1,180	1,562	1,731
Tamil Nadu	115	140	199	153
Tripura	Nil	Nil	18	3
Uttar Pradesh	4,102	4,279	3,865	3,977
West Bengal	02	33	23	17
Delhi	03	03	06	01
Goa, Daman & Diu	03	Nil	01	02
Arunachal Pradesh	02	Nil	Nil	Nil
Pondicherry	19	16	08	07
Total	13,975	13,866	14,308	15,054

Statistics about other States are Nil.

Annexure E 4

Comparative statement showing state-wise break-up of Atrocity cases committed on Scheduled Tribes during 1979, 1980, 1981 and 1982

State/Union Territory	Number of cases reported during			
	1979	1980	1981	1982
1	2	3	4	5
Andhra Pradesh	13	14	29	31
Bihar	200	101	174	85
Gujarat	72	93	95	104
Karnataka	20	1	5	04
Kerala	33	3	7	10
Madhya Pradesh	1.373	829	2.404	3.110
Maharashtra	181	146	232	213
Orissa	16	14	10	NA
Punjab	3	41	NA	NA
Rajasthan	205	308	386	472
Tamil Nadu	NA	NA	17	NA
West Bengal	NA	12	14	NA
Goa, Daman & Diu	1	NA	NA	00
Arunachal Pradesh	14	16	8	NA
Dadra & Nagar Haveli	3	NA	NA	01
Total	2.134	1.578	3.381	4.030

Statistics of other States were not available.

Source for E1 to E4 : V Report, of the Commission for Scheduled Castes and Scheduled Tribes.

Annexure F

Literacy Rates in 1971
For all Communites, Scheduled Cates, Scheduled tribes and all Communites (Excluding scheduled castes and scheduled tribes)

Sl. No.	India/State/Union Territory	All Communities	Scheduled Castes	Scheduled Tribes	All Communities excluding SC & ST
1	2	3	4	5	6
	INDIA	29.45	14.67	11.30	33.80
	STATES/U.Ts.				
1.	Andhra Pradesh	24.59	10.66	5.34	27.68
2.	Assam*	28.72	25.79	26.03	29.36
3.	Bihar	19.94	6.53	11.64	23.34
4.	Gujarat	35.79	27.74	14.12	40.31
5.	Haryana	26.98	12.60	—	30.22
6.	Himachal Pradesh	31.96	18.82	15.89	36.81
7.	Jammu & Kashmir	18.58	11.97	—	19.18
8.	Karnataka	31.52	13.89	14.85	34.36
9.	Kerala	60.42	40.21	25.72	62.76
10.	Madhya Pradesh	22.14	12.49	7.62	28.41
11.	Maharashtra	39.18	25.27	11.74	41.95
12.	Manipur	32.91	26.44	28.71	35.01
13.	Meghalaya	29.49	20.38	26.45	42.42
14.	Nagaland	27.40	—	24.01	53.78
15.	Orissa	26.18	15.61	9.46	35.02
16.	Punjab	33.67	16.12	—	39.42
17.	Rajasthan	19.07	9.14	6.47	23.38
18.	Sikkim	17.74	17.42	—	17.76
19.	Tamil Nadu	39.46	21.82	9.02	43.58
20.	Tripura	30.98	20.51	15.03	41.06
21.	Uttar Pradesh	21.70	10.20	14.59	24.79
22.	West Bengal	33.20	17.80	8.92	39.19
23.	Andaman & Nicobar Islands	43.59	—	17.85	48.40
24.	Arunachal Pradesh	11.29	36.28	5.20	34.23
25.	Chandigarh	61.56	24.38	—	66.30
26.	Dadra & Nagar Haveli	14.97	33.18	8.90	58.72
27.	Delhi	56.61	28.15	—	61.89
28.	Goa, Daman & Diu	44.75	26.14	12.73	45.41

1	2	3	4	5	6
29.	Lakshadweep	43.66	—	41.37	73.52
30.	Mizoram		Included	in Assam	
31.	Pondicherry	46.02	18.70	—	51.01

* Including Mizoram.
The percentages have been calculated on the total population inclusive of the popoulation in the age group of 0—4.
Source': Revision of Lists Cell, SC & BCD Division, Ministry of Home Affairs.

Source : Selected statistics on scheduled castes (1984) (occasional papers
: on develVpment of scheduled castes) MHA.

Annexure Fl

Literacy rates of Scheduled Castes/Scheduled Tribes and all communities for the year 1931, 1961, 1971 and 1981

Percentage of Literacy

	1931*	1951	1961●	1971*	1981*
Scheduled Castes	1.9	N.A.	10.3	14.8	21.4
Scheduled Tribes	0.7	N.A.	8.5	11.3	16.4
General (All communities)	9.5	16.7	24.0	29.5	36.2

Note :
* : Source : Selected statistics on Scheduled Castes, Ministry of Home Affairs.
● : Source : Report of the Commission for Scheduled Castes and Tribes (April 1981-March 1982-4th Report)

Annexure F2

Literacy rates of Scheduled Castes and Scheduled Tribes for the year 1961

States/Union Terribory	Scheduled Castes Percentage of Literates	Scheduled Tribes Percentage of Literates
Andhra Pradesh	8.5	4.4
Assam	24.4	23.5
Bihar	5.9	9.1
Gujarat	22.5	11.7
Haryana	--------CompositePunjab -----------	
Himachal Pradesh*	8.5	8.6
Jammu & Kashmir	5.0	—
Karnataka (Mysore)	9.1	7.9
Kerala	24.7	17.7
Madhya Pradesh	7.9	5.1
Maharashtra	15.8	7.2
Manipur*	22.4	27.2
Meghalaya	-------Composite Assam-----------	
Nagaland*	25.4	14.8
Orissa	11.6	7.4
Punjab	9.6	16.5
Rajasthan	6.4	4.0
Sikkim	—	—
Tamil Nadhu (Madras)	14.6	5.2
Tripura*	21.8	10.0
Uttar Pradesh	7.1	—
West Bengal	13.5	6.5
Andaman & Nicobar Islands	—	11.1
Arunachal Pradesh (NEFA)	—	30.0
Chandigarh	--------Composite Punjab----------	
D & N Haveli	22.1	4.4
Delhi	20.9	—
Goa, Daman & Diu	—	—
Lakshadweap	—	22.3
Mizoram	Composite Assam-----------	
Pondichery	11.1	—
All-India	10.3	8.5

Union Territories during the Consus year 1961

Annexure G

LITERACY RATES IN 1981

For All Communities, Scheduled castes, Scheduled tribes and all com-Munities excluding Scheduled castes and Scheduled tribes

Sl. No.	India/State/Union Territory	All Communities	Scheduled Castes	Scheduled Tribes	All communties excluding SC & ST
1	2	3	4	5	6
	INDIA	36.23	21.38	16.33	41.30
	STATES/U.Ts				
1.	Andhra Pradesh	29.94	17.64	7.82	33.91
2.	Assam	—	—	—	—
3.	Bihar	26.20	10.40	16.99	30.17
4.	Gujarat	43.70	39.78	21.14	48.14
5.	Haryana	36.14	20.14	—	39.90
6.	Himachal Pradesh	42.48	31.50	25.93	47.37
7.	Jammu & Kashmir	26.67	22.44	—	27.05
8.	Karnataka	38.46	20.59	20.14	42.95
9.	Kerala	70.42	55.96	31.79	75.32
10.	Madhya Pradesh	27.87	18.97	10.68	36.15
11.	Maharashtra	47.18	35.55	22.29	51.55
12.	Manipur	41.35	33.63	39.74	42.11
13.	Meghalaya	34.08	25.78	31.55	44.97
14.	Nagaland	42.57	—	40.31	54.39
15.	Orissa	34.23	22.41	13.96	44.22
16.	Punjab	40.86	23.86	—	47.11
17.	Rajasthan	24.38	14.04	10.27	29.31
18.	Sikkim	34.05	28.06	33.13	34.84
19.	Tamil Nadu	46.76	29.67	20.46	51.01
20.	Tripura	42.12	33.89	23.07	53.93
21.	Uttar Pradesh	27.16	14.96	20.45	30.45
22.	West Bengal	40.94	24.37	13.21	48.12
23.	Admand & Nicobar Islands	51.56	—	31.11	54.31

Sl. No.	India/State/Union Territory	All Communities	Scheduled Castes	Scheduled Tribes	All communities ex cluding S C & ST
1	2	3	4	5	6
24.	Arunachal Pradesh	20.79	37.14	14.04	36.39
25.	Chandigarh	64.78	37.07	—	69.33
26.	Dadra & Nagar Haveli	26.67	51.20	16.86	64.41
27.	Delhi	61.54	39.30	—	66.44
28.	Goa, Daman & Diu	56.66	38.38	26.48	57.38
29.	Laskshadweep	55.07	—	53.13	84.57
30.	Mizoram	59.88	84.44	59.63	63.53
31.	Pondichery	55.85	32.36	—	60.32

Source : Revision of Lists Cell, SC & BCD Division, Ministry of Home Affairs.
SOURCE : IBID

Annexure H

NO. OF POST MATRIC SCHOLARSHIPS AWARDED TO SCHEDULED CASTES AND SCHEDULED TRIBES STUDENTS

	Scheduled Castes		Scheduled Tribes	
Year	No. of Awards	Expenditure (Rs. in lakhs)	No. of Awards	Expenditure (Rs. in lakhs)
1951-52	1604	8.18	575	2.82
1961-62	49015	213.83	8548	36.78
1971-72	184565	956.00	27164	140.22
1981-82	553540	5285.08	104069	1015.19
1982-83	626242		119483	
1984-85	—	Total awards of scholarships		9,00,000 (approximately)

Source : Selected Statistics on Scheduled Castes
Occassional Papers on Development of
Scheduled Castes (2) (June' 1984)
Ministry of Home Affairs.

Annexure I

FACULTY-WISE GROWTH OF SC/ST ENROLMENT DURING THE YEAR 1978-79 AT GRADUATE LEVEL

Sl. No.	Faculty	Percentage of SC enrolment to total			Percentage of ST enrolment to total		
		1977-78	1978-79	Growth	1977-78	1978-79	Growth
1.	Arts	10.41	9.85	−0.56	2.04	2.48	+0.44
2.	Science	4.36	4.44	+0.08	0.82	0.83	+0.01
3.	Commerce	4.74	4.76	+0.02	1.27	1.27	—
4.	Education	6.07	6.24	+0.17	1.97	1.30	−0.67
5.	Engg./Tech.	6.07	6.16	+0.09	0.90	1.20	+0.30
6.	Medicine	8.37	9.98	+1.61	1.87	1.82	−0.05
7.	Agriculture	6.04	8.39	+2.35	0.45	0.71	+0.26
8.	Vet. Science	5.86	7.02	+1.16	1.36	1.14	−0.22
9.	Law	6.77	7.47	−0.70	1.85	1.32	−0.53
10.	Others	13.53	5.93	−7.60	0.54	0.42	−0.12
11.	Professional	6.80	7.45	+0.65	1.58	1.32	−0.26
12.	Non-Professional	7.70	7.30	−0.40	1.57	1.79	+0.22
	ALL INDIA	7.52	7.33	−0.19	1.57	1.70	+0.13

SOURCE OF : ANNEXURE I & J

Source : Report of the University Grents Commission on "Facilities to Scheduled Castes and Scheduled Tribes in Universites and Colleges"

Annexure J

FACULTY-WISE GROWTH OF SC/ST ENROLMENT DURING THE YEAR 1978-79 AT POSTGRADUATE LEVEL

Sl. No.	Faculty	Percentage of SC enrolment to total			Percentage of ST enrolment to total		
		1977-78	1978-79	Growth	1977-78	1978-79	Growth
1.	Arts	10.49	10.54	+0.05	1.71	1.93	+0.22
2.	Science	3.57	2.93	−0.64	0.71	0.79	+0.08
3.	Commerce	5.17	5.42	+0.25	1.04	1.29	+0.25
4.	Education	3.64	3.42	−0.22	1.03	0.68	−0.35
5.	Engg./Tech.	2.92	1.92	−1.00	0.53	0.18	−0.35
6.	Medicine	4.81	3.69	−1.12	0.72	0.50	−0.22
7.	Agriculture	2.79	4.48	+1.69	0.36	0.87	+0.51
8.	Veterinary Science	1.51	1.37	−0.14	—	—	—
9.	Law	1.84	3.97	+2.13	0.17	0.17	—
10.	Others	1.77	3.56	+1.79	0.40	0.56	+0.16
11.	Professional	3.52	3.45	−0.07	0.58	0.50	−0.08
12.	Non-Professiona l	8.09	8.17	+0.08	1.38	1.58	+0.20
	ALL INDIA	7.53	7.62	+0.09	1.28	1.46	+0.18

NUMBER OF APPLICANTS ON L.R. AT THE END OF

State	1978	1979	1980
Andhra Pradesh	982.7	1237.1	1442.2
Assam	286.7	319.2	314.7
Bihar	1503.7	1998.6	2294.0
Gujarat	397.1	420.4	469.9
Haryana	289.3	325.7	357.1
Himachal Pradesh	108.1	119.4	141.0
Jammu & Kashmir	47.4	52.7	51.4
Karnataka	536.6	553.9	597.1
Kerala	1051.7	1204.2	1579.1
Madhya Pradesh	756.4	737.5	826.7
Maharashtra	1008.5	1119.7	1229.8
Manipur	74.7	88.1	102.5
Meghalaya	10.4	10.3	9.8
Nagaland	3.2	4.3	5.1
Orissa	381.1	429.6	441.2
Punjab	384.6	407.6	452.6
Rajasthan	322.3	338.4	361.7
Sikkim*	—	—	—
Tamilnadu	967.1	987.6	1092.2
Tripura	68.3	70.8	70.9
Uttar Pradesh	1375.1	1407.6	1357.5
West Bengal	1749.0	2082.1	2536.4
UNION TERRITORIES			
Andaman & Nicobar Islands	6.8	8.1	9.5
Arunachal Pradesh*	—	—	—
Chandigarh	48.7	52.8	62.6
Dadra & Nagar Havelies**	—	—	—
Delhi	250.7	281.4	307.0
Goa	26.7	25.2	29.2
Lakshadweep	3.0	4.4	4.2
Mizoram	10.4	15.3	16.8
Pondicherry	27.4	32.0	38.0
India Total	12677.8	14333.9	16200.3

* No Employment Exchange is functioning.

** One Employment Exchange is functioning to this Union Territory, but data are not being received Minister of Labour, D.G. & T.

L.R. Live Register

Annexure-K

DECEMBER EACH YEAR (ALL CATEGORIES)

(In thousands)

1981	1982	1983	1984
1540.4	1764.8	2024.7	2172.8
371.4	399.9	476.4	487.1
2419.7	2556.3	2664.8	2668.5
533.9	580.2	580.5	631.8
325.0	446.8	438.5	467.6
159.3	169.0	186.2	257.6
55.9	61.7	70.4	66.7
629.4	684.4	735.4	770.0
1847.9	2029.6	2262.2	2529.1
882.2	913.0	1056.3	1115.4
1394.8	1551.3	1726.7	2100.4
132.6	149.1	167.5	186.0
10.4	9.8	10.9	11.9
8.5	8.6	10.5	13.4
488.1	481.8	536.3	559.4
486.0	505.5	530.8	526.2
396.2	404.2	465.1	504.7
—	—	—	—
1255.9	1392.0	1575.4	1706.5
82.8	79.1	83.1	92.7
1493.8	1610.4	1854.9	1873.2
2809.8	3438.2	3899.2	4124.2
10.9	12.1	10.4	11.7
—	—	—	—
68.9	75.4	83.2	88.3
—	—	—	—
289.7	328.7	389.8	451.2
31.8	33.0	34.3	43.0
4.8	5.3	5.7	6.3
15.6	14.0	19.4	16.7
42.9	48.6	55.0	64.0
17838.1	19753.0	21953.3	23546.0

Annexure KI

THE NUMBER OF JOB SEEKERS ON THE COUNTRY'S 800 EMPLOYMENT EXCHANGES ON DECEMBER 31, 1985

(In thousands)	Total	Women (included in total)
1 Below Matric (including illiterates)	12,294.5	
2 Matriculates	8,045.3	1,635.5
3 Persons who passed Higher Secondary (including Intermediates/under graduates)	3,530.4	623.9
4 Graduates (including Post-graduates)	2399.7	573.4
i) Arts	1,127.5	282.6
ii) Science	484.1	104.3
iii) Commarce	437.0	45.9
iv) Engineering	35.5	2.3
v) Medicine	23.3	5.2
vi) Veterinary	0.7	Not available
vii) Agriculture	25.9	0.3
viii) Law	10.5	0.9
ix) Education	225.9	123.3
x) Others	29.3	8.2
Total	26,270.0	2,832.8

Source : Illnstrated weekly November, 30 1986 Nikhil Lakshman : Despair, Frustration and Anger.

Annexure K2

HOW THE STATES AND UNION TERRITORIES FARED VIS-A-VIS UNEMPLOYMENT

	Region	No of applicants on the Live Register at the end of December, 1985 (in thousands)
	STATES	
1.	Andhra Pradesh	2328.8
2.	Assam	603.4
3.	Bihar	2549.5
4.	Gujarat	729.8
5.	Haryana	479.2
6.	Himachal Pradesh	314.5
7.	Jammu & Kashmir	73.9
8.	Karnataka	926.8
9.	Kerala	2573.5
10.	Madhya Pradesh	1429.0
11.	Maharashtra	2423.9
12.	Manipur	219.4
13.	Meghalaya	17.3
14	Nagaland	16.9
15.	Orissa	720.5
16.	Punjab	632.6
17.	Rajasthan	677.8
18.	Sikkim	Not available
19.	Tamil Nadu	2079.0
20.	Tripura	100.2
21.	Uttar Pradesh	2564.3
22.	West Bengal	3960.2

	Region	No of applicants on the Live Register at the end of December, 1985 (in thousands)
UNION TERRITORIES		
1.	Andaman & Nicobar Islands	12.4
2.	Arunachal Pradesh	Not available
3.	Chandigarh	112.2
4.	Dadra & Nagat Haveli	Not available
5.	Delhi	569.2
6.	Goa	50.5
7.	Lakshadweep	6.1
8.	Mizoram	23.6
9.	Pondicherry	75.6
	All India Total	26269.9

Source : Same as Kl

Annexure L

NO. OF EDUCATED SCHEDULED CASTES AND ALL CATEGORIES (INCLUDING SCHEDULED CASTES) ON LIVE REGISTER OF EMPLOYMENT EXCHANGES (AS ON 31.12.80) NO. ON LIVE REGISTER (1980)

	Educational Standard	Scheduled Castes	All Categories	Percentage Scheduled Castes on live register to all categories
1.	Matric	**413815**	**4568225**	9.06
2.	High Secondary	**182926**	**2070935**	8.83
3.	Graduates (Total)	**83844**	**1389771**	6.03
	i) Arts	55602	676016	8.22
	ii) Science	9349	310692	3.01
	iii) Engineering	205	22531	0.91
	iv) Medical	606	14809	4.09
4.	Post Graduates (Total)	**5395**	**134614**	4.01
	i) Arts	4013	78549	5.11
	ii) Science	497	25651	1.94
	iii) Engineering	9	1235	0.73
	iv) Medical	12	1836	0.65
5.	All Educated	685980	8163545	8.40

Scheduled caste job seekers on live register in some

Educational Standard	Bihar 1980	Bihar 1984	Gujarat 1980	Gujarat 1984
Matric	48330	67313	24859	36980
Higher Secondary	9787	17810	1565	4841
Graduate (Total)	5090	9994	1833	1952
i. Arts	3797	6611	1219	1130
ii. Science	744	2258	47	47
iii. Commerce	250	558	373	516
iv. Engineering	22	162	—	24
v. Medical	13	35	4	49
vi. Agriculture	14	15	10	14
vii. Law	3	11	5	5
viii. Education	179	274	151	150
ix. Others	68	72	24	17
Post Graduates (Total)	100	226	36	148
i. Arts	31	100	25	104
ii. Science	12	2	—	13
iii. Commerce	6	11	2	13
iv. Engineering	8	—	—	—
v. Medical	5	—	—	—
vi. Agriculture	4	—	—	—
vii. Law	—	—	—	—
viii. Education	26	17	9	4
ix. Others	8	96	—	14
Educated Total	63307	95343	28293	43921
Total S.C. on Live Register	158270	201109	64523	93897

Source : Ministry of Labour

Annexure M

selected states and All India during the years 1980 and 1984

States							
Karnataka		**Maharashtra**		**Uttar Pradesh**		**All- India**	
1980	**1984**	**1980**	**1984**	**1980**	**1984**	**1980**	**1984**
22318	31219	59362	92603	43887	60136	413815	672834
2231	3411	6020	10930	48906	60895	182926	262751
3749	4163	9566	13155	19292	30129	83844	118968
2199	2587	6427	7440	16310	22117	55602	72625
288	293	783	1356	936	3588	9349	18576
206	272	2249	3116	691	1537	9385	14213
13	187	6	127	20	55	205	1470
81	264	4	201	15	54	606	1394
48	127	16	107	199	585	453	1242
5	17	6	88	35	113	193	467
46	289	56	634	1028	2019	6413	8331
863	127	19	86	58	61	1638	650
229	748	167	2045	2089	3471	5395	12009
171	539	58	1258	1831	2975	4013	8430
47	179	17	150	97	111	497	1303
11	30	33	413	141	187	458	1133
—	—	—	—	—	—	9	4
—	—	1	1	—	—	12	17
—	—	7	6	5	18	39	33
—	—	2	—	—	2	14	3
—	—	37	49	8	172	262	683
—	—	12	168	7	6	91	403
28527	39541	75115	118733	114174	154631	685980	1066562
57686	77068	188741	280218	23659	294102	1815284	2617957

SCHEDULED TRIBES JOB SEEKERS ON LIVE RECISTER IN 1980 & 1984

Educational standard	Bihar		Gujarat	
	1980	1984	1980	1984
Matric	26020	33216	11474	15868
Higher Secondary	7686	9369	853	2938
Graduate (Total)	2798	6430	1720	1385
i. Arts	1862	4018	1116	816
ii. Commerce	141	785	188	278
iii. Science	446	1119	39	39
iv. Engineering	9	18	4	7
v. Medical	9	13	8	8
vi. Agriculture	39	11	49	32
vii. Law	1	13	—	2
viii. Education	275	430	310	173
ix. Others	16	23	10	30
Post Graduates (Total)	96	126	16	50
i. Arts	48	59	12	31
ii. Commerce	3	11	—	2
iii. Science	16	11	1	7
iv. Engineering	—	—	—	1
v. Medical	—	—	—	—
vi. Agriculture	—	—	—	1
vii. Law	—	—	—	—
viii. Education	22	30	1	1
ix. Others	7	15	2	9
Educated Total	36600	49441	14063	20243
Total S.T. on Live Register	116910	132147	31227	38516

Source : Ministry of Labour

SOME SELECTED STATES AND ALL-INDIA DURING THE YEAR,

STATES							
Karnataka		Maharashtra		Uttar Pradesh		All-India	
1980	1984	1980	1984	1980	1984	1980	1984
3368	3372	11182	17811	517	698	91124	153330
478	654	1266	2226	461	675	40049	53562
558	511	1155	1833	119	279	13202	22449
309	262	621	930	90	194	9165	14926
46	51	407	503	4	20	1355	2793
86	63	98	272	18	48	1238	2408
9	12	3	22	—	—	34	161
2	25	2	39	—	—	79	205
—	10	4	19	—	—	107	109
3	—	2	2	—	—	21	48
24	70	18	92	6	17	941	1551
79	18	—	4	1	—	262	248
44	143	10	119	17	68	803	2220
30	92	7	60	17	48	600	1512
—	5	—	35	—	12	39	187
14	39	1	15	—	3	112	318
—	—	—	—	—	—	—	8
—	—	—	—	—	—	—	10
—	—	—	—	—	—	1	2
—	—	2	1	—	—	2	2
—	—	—	1	—	5	37	110
—	7	—	7	—	—	12	71
4448	4680	13613	22039	1114	1720	145178	231561
6499	8465	37274	53853	1932	3262	475707	659606

Annexure O

EMPLOYMENT OF SCHEDULED CASTES AND SCHEDULED TRIBES IN VARIOUS CLASSES OF SERVICES UNDER CENTRAL GOVERNMENT

Year	Class-I		Class-II		Class-III		Class-IV	
	S.C.	S.T.	S.C.	S.T.	S.C.	S.T.	S.C.	S.T.
1970	593	100	1513	147	130803	20811	218034	43248
	(2.36)	(0.40)	(3.84)	(0.37)	(9.27)	(1.47)	(18.09)	(3.59)
1975	1197	219	2689	321	174025	36859	230811	49439
	(3.44)	(0.63)	(5.00)	(0.60)	(10.66)	(2.26)	(18.64)	(3.99)
1980	2311	499	4662	717	200324	52830	245971	68075
	(4.83)	(1.04)	(8.07)	(1.24)	(11.54)	(3.04)	(19.16)	(5.30)

Note : 1) Figures in bracket indicates percent to total employment
2) DGP&T—Figures excludes extra departmental workers and Industrial workers.
3) Class—IV excludes sweepers.
4) S.C. - Scheduled Castes
S.T. - Scheduled Tribes

Source : 1970 & 1975 - Social Information of India trends & Structure.
1980 - Report of the Commission for Scheduled Castes and Scheduled Tribes (2nd Report).

Annexure P

STATEMENT SHOWING THE POSITION ABOUT RECRUITMENT OF CANDIDATES BELONGING TO SCHEDULED CASTES/SCHEDULED TRIBES AGAINST VACANCIES RESERVED FOR THEM ON THE RESULTS OF THE EXAMINATION HELD DURING : 1968 to 1972

Name of examination	Year	Scheduled Castes			Schedduled Tribes		
		No. of vacancies reserved-ved	No. of candidates		No. of vacan-cies	No. of candidates	
			Appeared ed	Recom-mended		Appear-ed	Recom-mmened
1	2	3	4	5	6	7	8
Indian Administrative Service etc. Examination	1968	50*	1198	50	19*	300	19
	1969	54*	1299	54	23*	316	23
	1970	65*	1286	65	28*	266	28
	1971	93*	1313	93	46*	307	34
	1972	91*	1626	91	56*	359	41
Indian Forest Service Examination	1968	5	142	5	2	41	2
	1969	2	96	2	1	21	1
	1970	3	96	3	—	18	—
	1971	2	82	2	1	13	1
	1972	2	89	2	1	26	1

1	2	3	4	5	6	7	8
Engineering Services Examination	1986	55	82	13	27	6	—
	1969	45	98	27	22	7	4
	1970	47	102	17	28	10	1
	1971	57	96	14	29	6	1
	1972	77	148	38	49	8	1
Engineering Services (Electronics) Examination	1968		No Examination was		held		
	1969	9	8	2	5	—	—
	1970	15	4	2	3	—	—
	1971	29	11	4	15	1	1
	1972	49	9	2	22	—	—

* Includes vacancies remaining unfilled on the results of the corresponding examination for Released Emergency Commissioned/Short Service Commissioned Officers.

Source :
Twenty third report
UPSC (April 1, 1972 to March 3, 1973)

Annexure Q

STATEMENT SHOWING THE POSITION ABOUT RECRUITMENT OF SCHEDULED CASTE/SCHEDULED TRIBES AGAINST VACANCIES RESERVED FOR THEM ON THE RESULTS OF THE EXAMINATIONS HELD DURING THE YEAR 1979 TO 1983

Name of Examination	Year	Number of Vacancies	Scheduled Castes Number of Candidates		Number of Vacancies	Scheduled Tribes Number of Candidates	
		reserved	Appeared	Recommended	reserved	Appeared	Recommended
Civil Services (Main) Examination	1979	112	1139	112	80	723	80
	1980	131	1426	131	75	824	75
	1981	144	1417	144	79	764	79
	1982	157	1445	157	82	756	82
	1983	*	1743	**	*	926	**
Indian Forest Services Examination	1979	15	223	15	7	199	9
	1980	15	313	15	8	109	8
	1981	18	343	18	9	110	9
	1982	18	323	18	9	103	9
	1983	23	294	21	11	114	9
Engineering Services Examination	1979	169	297	135	105	30	18
	1980	124	324	130	96	28	17
	1981	191	380	145	112	34	18
	1982	178	428	120	106	48	22
	1983	*	426	**	*	55	**
Combined Examination for recruitment to Medical Posts under the Central Government	1979	120	721	154***	148	115	35
	1980	157	720	218****	182	114	49
	1981	86	845	92*****	64	137	50
	1982	77	1382	77	48	261	48
	1983	138	1158	138	77	230	77

Note

* Final figures not yet received from Government.

** Results not announced by 31-3-1984

*** Includes 34 candidates recommended against vacancies reserved for Scheduled Tribe candicate

**** Includes 81 candidates recommended against vacancies reserved for scheduled Tribe candidates

***** Includes 6 candidates recommended against vacancies reserved for Scheduled Tribes candidates.

Rastogi, P.N.	India 1981-86 : A forecaste on Economic, Political and Social Developments.	50.00
Khanna, Rita	Agricultural Mechanisation and Social Change in India.	125.00
Shrivastava, M.P.	Problems of Accountability of Public Enterprises in India.	250.00
Roy, R.C., *IAS*	State Public Enterprise in India.	200.00
Wishwakarama, R.K.	Urban and Regional Planning Policy in India.	75.00

EDUCATION

Bayti, Jamnalal	Problems of Education in the third world.	200.00
Bayti, Jamnalal	Readings in Education.	150.00
Paliwal, M.R.	Differential Effectiveness of Micro-learning.	50.00
Paliwal, M.R.	Social Change and Education.	175.00
Paliwal, M.R.	The Teacher Education on the Move : Today and Tomorrow.	225.00

HISTORY

Anderson, G. & Subedar, M.	The Expansion of British India (1818-1858).	150.00
Aspinall, A.	Cornwallis in Bengal.	200.00
Biswas, Atreyi	Political, Social and Cultural History of Ancient India (H).	125.00
May, L.S.	The Evolution of Indo-Muslim Thought from 1857 to Present.	250.00
Madan, J.C.	Indian Police.	110.00
Mohanta, Bijan	Administrative Development of Arunachal Pradesh 1875-1975.	150.00

Rawlinson, H.G.	Indian Historical Studies.	200.00
Sikka, R.P.	The Civil Service in India.	150.00

LAW

Ahangar, Mohd. Altaf Hussain	Customary Succession Among Muslims.	175.00
Chaudhari, R.L.	The Concept of Secularism in Indian Constitution	150.00
Jagannadham, V.	Administration and Social Change.	60.00
Saksena, H.S.	Safeguards for Scheduled Castes and Tribes : Founding Father's View.	200.00
Singh, S.S.	Administration of Natural Justice in India.	250.00

LIBRARY SCIENCE

Pandey, S.K. Sharma	Dewey Decimal Classification for Indology.	200.00
Rajjan Lal and Kidwai, Nasira	Practical Cataloguing Procedure (Hindi).	95.00

POLITICAL SCIENCE

Baruah, A.K.	Systems Analysis in Political Science : A Marxit Critique of David Easton.	125.00
Chaudhari, R.L.	The Concept of Secularism in Indian Constitution.	150.00
Gabriel, Soloman	Foreign Policy of Canada	95.00
Ghosh, Partha S.	Sino-Soviet Relations : U.S. Perception and Policy Resp.	100.00
Kaushik, S.N.	Pakistan under Bhutto's Leadership.	175.00
Mahendra Singh	Indo-U.S. Relations : A Political Study.	75.00

Mishra, Upendra	Caste and Politics in India.	225.00
Mukarji, Nirmal and Ashis Banerjee	Democracy Federalism and the future of Indias Unity	60.00
Pai Panandiker, V.A. and Arun Sud.	Changing Political Representation in India.	65.00
Pal, J.J.	Jinnah and the creation of Pakistan.	75.00
Pandey, Jawaharlal	State Politics in India.	90.00
Pillai, G. Narayana	Social Background of Political Leadership in India.	90.00
Pirzada, Syed Sharifuddin	Evolution of Pakistan.	175.00
Rao, V. Bhaskara,	General Elections in India.	150.00
Reddy, P. Ranjani	The Role of Dominant Caste in Indian Politics.	125.00
Seshadri, K.	Studies in Indian Polity.	150.00
Seshadri, K.	Studies in the problems of the third world.	175.00
Sharma, T.R.	New Challenges in Indian Politics.	175.00
Singh, L.P. *ICS*	Electoral Reform : Problems and Suggested Solutions.	95.00
Singh, L.P.	India's Foreign Policy.	55.00
Singh, S.P.	Perspectives in Indian Politics and Administration.	60.00
Verma, S.P.	Indian Parliamentarians : A Study of the Socio-Political Background.	90.00
Vijay Kumar	India and Srilanka-China Relations 1948-84.	125.00

PUBLIC ADMINISTRATION

Banerjea, Pramathanath	Public Administration in Ancient India.	125.00

Bawa, Noorjahan	People's Participation Development Adm. in India.	125.00
Bhattacharjee, Debasish	Bureacracy and Development in Meghalaya.	150.00
Bhattacharya, Mohit	Bureaucracy and development Administration.	50.00
Bhattacharya, Mohit	Management of Urban Government in India	50.00
Bijan Mohanta	Administrative Development of Arunachal Pradesh, 1875-1975.	150.00
Dey, Bata K.	Bureaucracy Development and Public Management in India.	80.00
Jagannadham, V.	Administration and Social Change.	60.00
Jain, R.B. and P.N. Chaudhuri	Bureaucratic Values in Development.	120.00
Jain, R.B.	Comparative Legislative Behaviour.	50.00
Padhi, A.P. and Mishra, S.N.	State Administration in India. (in 2 Vols.)	350.00
Panda, Basudev	Indian Bureaucracy : An Inside Story.	60.00
Partap Singh	Urban Government in India.	45.00
Rai, Haridwar and S.P. Singh	Current Ideas and Issues in Indian Administration.	70.00
Sharma, P.D.	Police and Criminal Justice Administration in India.	125.00
Sharma, P.D.	Police, Polity and People in India.	125.00
Sikka, R.P.	The Civil Service in India.	150.00
Singh, L.P. *ICS*	Sardar Patel and Indian Administration.	30.00
Singh, S.S.	Administration of Natural Justice in India.	250.00

Sundeep Khanna, *IAS*	Civil Administration in India.	60.00
Trivedi, B.V.	Prison Administration in India : Model Prison Programme.	120.00
Wishwakarma, R.K.	Urban and Regional Planning Policy in India.	75.00

SOCIOLOGY

Ahangar, Mohd. Altaf Hussain	Customary Succession Among Muslims.	175.00
Amir Hussain, *IAS*	A Tribe in Turmoil : Socio-Economic Study of Jammu Gujars of Uttar Pradesh.	150.00
Brett-Crowther, M.R.	Brandt, Bread and the Bomb : Reflexions on the World Problematic.	90.00
Bawa, Noor Jahan	People's Participation Development Administration in India	125.00
Centre for Policy Research, N. Delhi	Population, Poverty and hope.	300.00
Chaudhari, R.L.	The Concept of Secularism in Indian Constitution.	150.00
Durrany, K.S.	Religion in Society.	200.00
Ghosh, Shubhra	Female Criminals in India.	125.00
Jagannadham, V.	Administration and Social Change.	60.00
Kamble, N.D.	Bonded Labour in India.	60.00
Kamble, N.D.	Migrants in Indian Metropolis.	75.00
Khan, Mumtaz Ali	Scheduled Caste and their Status in India.	75.00
Khan, Mumtaz Ali	Status of Rural Women in India.	75.00
Khan, Mumtaz Ali	Social Legislation and the Rural Poor.	50.00
Khan, Mumtaz Ali	Muslims in the Process of Rural Development in India.	50.00

Krishnakumari, N.S.	Status of Single Women in India.	125.00
Mandal, B.B.	Tribals at the Polls : A Study of Khunti in Chotanagpur.	90.00
Madan, J.C.	Indian Police.	110.00
Menon, M. Indu	Status of Muslim Women in India.	50.00
Mishra, Upendra	Caste and Politics in India.	225.00
Mishra, S.N. and Kushal Sharma	Problems and Prospects of Rural Development in India.	80.00
Mohan, N. Shantha	Status of Nurses in India.	60.00
Paliwal, M.R.	Social Change and Education.	175.00
Pai Panandikar, V.A. and Ajay K. Mehra	People's Participation in Family Planning.	160.00
Pai Panandiker, V.A., R.N. Bisnnoi and O.P. Sharma	Organisational Policy for Family Planning.	125.00
Pai Panandiker, V.A. and P.N. Chaudhuri	Demographic Transition in Goa and its Policy Implications.	40.00
Pandey, K.K.	Rural Development in India : Continuity and Change.	125.00
Pillai, G. Narayana	Social Background of Political Leadership in India.	90.00
Rajgopal, P.R.	Communal Violence in India.	140.00
Rastogi, P.N.	India 1981-86 : A forecaste on Economic, Political and Social Developments.	50.00
Ray, B. Datta	The Emergence and Role of Middle Class in North East India.	100.00
Ray, B. Datta	The Pattern and Problems of Population in North-East India.	250.00
Rita Khanna	Agricultural Mechanisation and Social Change in India.	125.00

Saksena, H.S.	Safeguards for Scheduled Castes and Tribes : Founding Father's View.	200.00
Seshadri, K.	Studies in Indian Polity.	150.00
Seshadri, K.	Studies in the Problems of the Third World.	175.00
Sharma, P.D.	Police and Criminal Justice Administration in India.	125.00
Sharma, P.D.	Police, Polity and People in India.	125.00
Sharma, R.N. & Santosh Bakshi	Tribes and Tribal Development : Select Bibliography.	250.00
Sinha, R.P.	Social Dimensions of Trade Unionism in India.	90.00
Singh, K.P.	Tribal Development in India.	250.00
Singh, S.S.	Administration of Natural Justice in India.	250.00
Singh, S.S. and S. Sundram	Emerging Harijan Elite : A Study of their Identity.	125.00
Trivedi, B.V.	Prison Administration in India.	120.00
Wishwakarma, R.K.	Urban and Regional Planning Policy in India.	75.00

REFERENCE BOOKS

Desmukh, C.D.	Amarakosa : Gems from the Treasure House of Sanskrit Words.	90.00
Durrany, K.S.	Religions in Society : Select Indian Press Index of Comparative Religion.	200.00
Pandey, S.K. Sharma	Dewey Decimal Classification for Indology.	200.00
Sharma, R.N. and Santosh Bakshi	Tribes and Tribal Development : Select Bibliography.	250.00